PRINCE

PRINCE

—by Steven Ivory—

A PERIGEE BOOK

PERIGEE BOOKS
are published by
The Putnam Publishing Group
200 Madison Avenue
New York, NY 10016

LIBRARY OF CONGRESS CATALOGING IN PUBLICATION DATA

Ivory, Steven.
Prince.

"A Perigee book."
1. Prince.   2. Rock musicians—Biography.
I. Title.
ML420.P974I9   1985   784.5'4'00924   [B]   84-17872
ISBN 0-399-51141-5 (pbk.)

PRINTED IN THE UNITED STATES OF AMERICA
1   2   3   4   5   6   7   8   9   10

Acknowledgments

While I could go on for pages thanking the many people who ultimately contributed to this exhaustive project, there are some very special people whom I must acknowledge: Journalists Robert Hilburn, Miles White, Debby Miller, Jeffrey Jolson-Colburn, Jon Bream, Barbara Graustark, Leo Sacks, Lee Bailey and *Radioscope*. Special thanks to comrade Nelson George for introducing me to the project. Thanks to Denise Hall for connecting me with my "secret" agents Bart Andrews and Sherry Robb: thank you for your professionalism, love and clippings. Thank you Pat Charbonnet, Owen Husney, Micki Free, André Cymone, Dez Dickerson, Roger Glazer, Laurel Sylvanus, Lorrie Janson and Kathe Duba-Noland at Warner Bros., my editors, Joe Pheifer and Adrienne Ingrum; Ronda Robinson for the fan and Gina Bolton for much needed assistance beyond the call of duty. *Special* thanks to Charles Smith. Pasta by Intermezzo on Melrose. I'd like to meet the man who invented NoDoz.

I appreciate your contribution: Raymond Burch, Delight Hanover, Bobby Holland, John Ivory, The Ivory Family, Regina Jones, Bob Jones, the Minnises, the Lewises, Jessie Turner and her wonderful daughters, Gary Taylor and everyone from 6th and High. Thank you James T. McDonough, for sharing with me The Power.

Prince: Whatever it is, you've got it; whatever it takes you give it. And that's how you did it. Thanks.

FOR MARJORIE

Contents

1.

Prince Rogers Nelson

To be sure, it was the hottest ticket in Hollywood. To possess an invitation to Prince's *Purple Rain* movie premiere was to be on Hollywood's "A" list, if for only one night. In charge of a guest list so long that certain celebrities were being denied entry, officials at Warner Bros. Pictures, the company that distributed the movie, spent the eve of the premiere playing God, deciding who was important enough to be there and who would spend the night looking at the event on MTV, which had negotiated for the right to broadcast the party live.

Those lucky enough to be invited were themselves in awe. Ray Parker, Jr., a pop/R&B singer with a Top-10 hit record at the time—"Ghostbusters"—was pulling all stops. He got Joe Ruffalo, one of his managers as well as one of Prince's, to contact Selection Import/ Export, which maintains a stable of exotic cars, and arrange for the use of a rare white Mercedes Gull Wing, valued at about $150,000. If Parker could help it, there'd be no way his arrival at Mann's Chinese Theatre would go unnoticed by *Entertainment Tonight* cameras or the throngs of fans who lined Hollywood Boulevard to experience the whole thing.

Micki Free, the pretty-boy guitarist from the pop/rock group Shalamar, was thinking likewise. He had his tailor whip up a two-piece lipstick-red suede number especially for the occasion. When he squeezed into it, he resembled a hip matador wearing mascara and earrings. Of course, like Parker, Lionel Ritchie, Steven Spielberg, Eddie Murphy, Morgan Fairchild, Christopher Reeve, Quincy Jones, Stevie Nicks, Little Richard (toting a Bible as a gift for Prince) and a host of others springing from a train of limousines, Free was dead wrong. How, especially tonight, could anyone have possibly outhazed a veritable master of haze? From 7 P.M. on, Hollywood belonged to His Royal Baddness, an enigmatic five-foot-three musician from Minneapolis named Prince.

Actually, the glamour-ridden spectacle unfolding on Hollywood Boulevard that night was a movie premiere that symbolized something more, though it was most appropriate that it be going on here, at the majestic Chinese Theatre, where the footprints of a legion of Hollywood stars stand forever preserved in the sidewalk.

The fact is, Prince is living something far more interesting than anything portrayed on the silver screen. Cecil B. DeMille, the legendary movie director, couldn't have made a better rags-to-riches tale of a kid growing up in the midwest, yearning to be a star. He becomes proficient on guitar, keyboards and drums, and sets out to conquer the world. Ironically, the kid, product of a troubled childhood, is driven by something he deems bigger than mere superstardom; his quest is simply to *belong*, to be somebody, not to the world as much as to his family and friends and enemies all trapped in this lackluster region of America.

Instead of moving away to the bright lights of some vast metropolis, the kid stays and rules the town as king, or more accurately, Prince. And like such a *Star Is Born* saga, the *Purple Rain* night wasn't without its dramatic scenarios—for example, the in-camp battling going on even as the movie's premiere drew nearer.

13

Or the fact that at what had to be one of the most spectacular moments in Prince's life, the star seemed lonely, removed and indifferent.

Prince is the most invigorating thing to happen to rock music since Michael Jackson's *Thriller* became the largest-selling album in the history of recorded music. Of course, the comparisons between these two artists were inevitable. Each is a reclusive, young, Black, androgynous mesh of musical talent and perception that, at its best, often approaches brilliance. That, however, is where the similarities end. If Jackson, because of his mass appeal and burgeoning record sales, is the new king of pop, then Prince is his more adventurous counterpart, waiting to ascend the throne.

Prince built a career on risqué, if not downright nasty, songs that take artistic freedom to the limits. He tapped the surging sexuality of our times and composed songs that weaved intriguing scenes around casual, often hardcore, sex. His dynamic stage shows frequently ended with Prince in nothing more than legwarmers, bikini underwear and a layer of perspiration. Jackson's fashion trademark became an oversized sequined glove, not totally unlike something Mickey Mouse would wear; Prince, on the other hand, adopted a trench

14

coat, generally recognized as a pervert's calling card; the color of his coat is purple.

As late as *1999*, the two-record set released in 1982 that until the *Purple Rain* soundtrack was his biggest recorded success, Prince was having passionate, vivid sex on wax, explicitly describing what he wanted to do with a chance encounter.

In short, the *Purple Rain* premiere was in reality the celebration of an artist who achieved success on his own terms, who bought his hybrid of steamy funk grooves, edgy rock guitar and erotic lyrics from the anonymity of Minneapolis music clubs to a mainstream Hollywood movie premiere, replete with famous peers, screaming fans, and paparazzi jockeying for a clear shot and national news coverage.

Prince had become a star.

At exactly 7:30 P.M., after most of the other guests had made their entrances, a long purple limousine aligned itself with the red carpet that extended to the curb in front of the theater. Emerging almost immediately was Chick, the humongous, white-haired bodyguard, himself now famous as his employer's constant menacing shadow. Right behind Chick came the person the crowd had been waiting for since they'd gathered more than three hours earlier: Prince. Wearing a shiny purple trench coat and equally flashy rock 'n' roll duds underneath, Prince was the essence of the rude, cocky royalty that is his image.

His eyes danced nervously as he was ushered up the runway. For the people outside the theater, Prince's rather uneventful entry marked the end of an evening. For Prince, striding into the elegant movie house without so much as a wave to the crowd, it signaled the beginning of a new, crowning occupation: Superstar.

Prince Rogers Nelson was born June 7, 1958. That makes him two years older than the previously published age. Prince's real age has been just one of the mysteries surrounding the musician. He was born in Minneapolis to Mattie and John Nelson, two people whose completely opposite personalities are reflected in Prince's own dual personality.

Mattie is a light-skinned Black woman who migrated to the midwest from Baton Rouge, Louisiana. Still an attractive woman today, she and her sister, Edna Mae, were, when they came to Minneapolis, easily two of the most beautiful women in the city. Mattie was hip. Depending on who you talk to, Mattie and Edna were anything from "fast" to simply girls who knew how to have a good time.

"In those days, Mattie was a carefree sort of person," said one who remembers. "She had a fun-loving heart."

One of Prince's childhood friends recalled that Mattie and Edna "were always looking good. Their hair was always dyed blond or red or something like that, and their faces were always made up. The women today don't have anything on them. They were wearing the 'Marilyn Monroe look' *out*, even back then."

John Nelson, on the other hand, was quiet, soft-spoken. A thin, handsome man of medium height, John wore his slightly processed hair combed back. He drove a white 1966 Thunderbird, which he kept in mint condition. To support his family, he worked as a plaster molder at the local Honeywell plant, but his life was really as a musician. He was an accomplished piano player and composer whose musical forte was an elegant kind of smoky-room jazz. His combo, the Prince Rogers Band, gigged in the local Minneapolis spots. John's own compositions were like him—somber, eclectic, *different*.

From the beginning, the combination of John and Mattie was an unlikely one. Mattie was a woman who loved to live, loved to have *fun*. She liked to dance; she liked to go out. John was a very serious man. Serious about his ambitions as a musician, serious about life. Ultimately, their opposite personalities came into conflict.

In the beginning, though, things were fine. Mattie was also a musician—a torch singer in the style of Billie Holiday—and she sang with John's band until she married him. Two years later, when she gave birth to the first of the two kids she and John had, the child was named Prince Rogers Nelson, after the group. (Titles as names, suggesting official authority, seemed to be a hallmark of the Nelson family. Years later, Tyka, Prince's sister, named her two sons Sir and President.) However, family and friends came to call Mattie and John's son Skipper, mainly because that's what his mother called him "because he was so small and cute" but also because Prince himself didn't care for his real name. When he was a child, anyone consistently calling him Prince was looking for a fight.

Prince's first ten years of life were fairly ordinary. With both parents musically inclined, it was little wonder that Prince was naturally attracted to music. Midwest radio at the time largely consisted of Top-40 stations that played very little Black music, only whatever Black artists made the national Top 10, like the Motown sound, some James Brown and a sparse amount of stuff from the Stax roster. Thus, Prince came up largely on a musical diet of Beatles, Rolling Stones, Jimi Hendrix, and Sly and the Family Stone. It is the same musical repertoire on which Prince bases his songs today.

Generally, Prince was a pleasant child, though his close friends were few. At Bryant Junior High, he got good grades and hung out with the jocks. In fact, despite his size, Prince was one hell of a basketball player on the team at Bryant. He developed into a good shooter, and his size allowed him to steal the ball often. He divided any social life between basketball and music. He enrolled in a guitar class, took some courses in music theory, song copyrighting and the music business. It was an area Prince would later learn to manipulate shrewdly.

In any case, Prince wasn't exactly a recluse. He had cronies; they'd jock around together and "play the dozens"—street slang for talking about each other's parents. In many ways, his life was as ordinary as that of any child approaching his teens.

Still, few people ever really penetrated

Prince's thick protective emotional shield. That is, until André Anderson. Anderson first met Prince in their junior high school gym class. Anderson, new at the school, was being reprimanded by the gym teacher and was told to stand up against the wall. There were other boys already holding it up; one of them was Prince. "We just started talking, and that was it. After that, we just sort of hung out together every day."

Prince and André actually had more of a link than they first realized. Once, while visiting Prince's home, André noticed a band picture on John Nelson's piano. He instantly recognized the bass musician next to the piano player in the picture. "It was my father. I couldn't believe it, because Prince and I immediately got on so well, and here we had something else in common. It was deep." According to Prince's father, Prince and André actually first met when the two were babies. Just as their fathers shared a band, so one day would Prince and André.

In the meantime, that unlikely combination of John and Mattie had begun slowly to unravel. By the time Prince was in his teens, it was clear that the marriage wouldn't last much longer. They argued often and sometimes had fights. By the time Prince turned thirteen, his parents had divorced. Not long after, Mattie remarried.

Prince disliked the fact that John and Mattie couldn't stay together almost as much as he disliked Haywood Baker, his new stepfather. Haywood was a no-frills man who was interested in Mattie but had a difficult time relating to her children. By now, Prince, on guitar, and André, on bass, were playing together in a band called Grand Central, which had been formed by Prince's second cousin, Charles Smith, who played drums. It was Prince's first band, and although Grand Central was composed of children all about thirteen years old, it was a serious situation. It also featured André's sister Linda on keyboards and Terry Jackson, later replaced by William Daughty, on percussion.

Smith recalls that Haywood immediately made his presence felt. "It affected me, because Prince and I used to hang out together, and Haywood started putting Prince on these long punishments, which would keep him from rehearsals. He would tell Prince he could go rehearse after he picked all the dandelions out of the backyard and stuff like that. The dandelions would grow back the next day."

Soon Mattie's relationship with Haywood

21

began to sour as well. They would have arguments. Fights. Prince has related that his stepfather punished him by grounding him to his room for weeks. The only things in the room were a bed and a piano, so he taught himself to play the piano. He was so miserable, he ran away to live with his father, who stayed nearby.

Prince always wanted to get closer to his dad, but both seemed to have difficulty sharing their feelings. Still, they got along fine in John's small home until one day John came in and found Prince with a girl in his room. From that day on, Prince's father ruled him with a steadier hand, like Haywood, cramping Prince's free, independent lifestyle. Prince refused to go back to live in the same house with Haywood; and a stint with an aunt simply didn't work out. The only thing left to do was move in with André Anderson's family.

Bernadette Anderson, André's mother, already faced the task of raising six kids, including André. Raising yet *another* seemed an unnecessary burden to take on, but Bernadette wasn't exactly a stranger to the situation. Herself a divorcée, she understood the problems Mattie and Prince were having. After all, Prince's father once made music with Bernadette's ex-husband. Prince was like family.

For Prince, adopting the Andersons simply meant his family tree extended even further. When his parents divorced, they each married people who had also been divorced and had children. As it was, in addition to Tyka, through Mattie's second marriage alone, Prince gained young Omar, a half brother, and two step-siblings. From his father's second union came four half and stepbrothers and sisters. There was also Duane Nelson, a half brother near Prince's age from John's relationship before Mattie. Prince refers to him in the song "Lady Cab Driver" from the album *1999* and in his handful of interviews as the "taller" brother of whom he grew jealous.

From a musical standpoint, the living arrangement couldn't have been better. André, Prince and his cousin Charles could now spend as much time as they wanted making music. Bernadette was fairly permissive with the fellas. As long as they went to school, got good grades and stayed out of trouble, they could do whatever they wanted.

Initially, André and Prince tried sharing André's room. As André told *Rock Magazine*, "We were separate people, and we wanted to divide the room to prove it. So I took a piece of tape and put it in the center of the floor and up the walls. My side was packed with junk; clothes, T-shirts, guitars, you name it. Prince's side was immaculate. His clothes were always folded and hung up. He even made his bed every day!"

Still, the two were constantly debating over territory; Prince decided he'd move to the basement of the house. There he'd be able to play guitar anytime he wanted. He put up a big full-length mirror so he could look at his compact but well-built frame. Most importantly, down here Prince would be able to have a semblance of privacy, something that has always been vital to his mental make-up. He put the last of his belongings into a corner, collapsed on the bed and uttered a sigh of relief. Prince's infamous basement years were about to begin.

2.

Minneapolis to New York

Minneapolis is a peculiar portion of the United States. It is one of the few places in the country that can be whatever you want it to be. It can possess a cosmopolitan aura, like a midwestern San Francisco. On the other hand, its wide open fields have been Marlboro country for many a retiree. It *can* be those things and more. However, in reality, this is a community where, unlike Manhattan, most people live in houses not apartments and where, unlike Los Angeles, people have real backyards. With clotheslines in them. Minnesota, in many ways, is the archetype of the American Heartland.

This relative calm—the kind of everything-is-all-right stillness that graces a small town being invaded by discreet aliens in B-rated science fiction movies—had to have affected the fervor with which Prince worked to get out of his town or at least be somebody in it. By now, Grand Central had slowly worked its way up to a reputation as one of the best bands on Minneapolis's north side. Prince was spending less time with sports—he ultimately quit Central High School's basketball team altogether—and more time with music. He seemed to have a natural ability with any instrument he spent enough time with.

Fellow classmates recall how Prince would sneak into a class he wasn't enrolled in, pick up any instrument and work out on it for a while with the rest of the class until he either left on his own or was asked out by an irate teacher. That is the way Prince became acquainted with more than twenty musical instruments: by watching others play them, imitating their actions and adding his own.

Grand Central hit all the usual garage band outlets. They played the YMCA, the community centers, high school sock-hops and talent shows. Always a second-string man when it came to sports, Prince had finally found his niche. As he told the Los Angeles *Times* in a 1982 interview with Robert Hilburn, "My older brother was the basketball and football star. He always had all the girls around him and stuff like that. I think I must have been on a jealous trip, because I got out of sports. I wasn't bad at basketball, but my brother was better, and he wouldn't let me forget it. When I did get a band, the first thing I did was bring it to school, play the homecoming dance and say, 'Look at *this*.' It was something they couldn't do."

At the center of Grand Central was the cohesive combination of Prince on guitar and André on bass. Musically, they were fast becoming the dynamic duo of Minneapolis. "Prince and André could wear anybody out," says Charles Smith, who, in addition to being drummer, says he sang a lead falsetto most of the time. "The interaction of their guitar and bass work was more than anybody could stand. Musically, they had the kind of sixth sense that twins have. They would just smoke."

Prince and his father may not have seen eye to eye domestically, but John avidly supported his son's musical efforts. He bought Prince his first guitar—a piano was too expensive—and he'd often come to Grand Central's local sets. "I remember him to be there most of the time," says Smith. "I remember one gig we had at the YMCA. It didn't happen very much, but for whatever reason, not very many people came to the show. But there was Prince's father with this camera, taking pictures just like the place was packed. He was intense about it, too, taking pictures from all angles."

Bernadette Anderson was even more supportive. She was the one who had to listen to the music seeping up from her basement through the floorboards, generally at all hours. Somehow, she seemed to understand their diligence was a sign of more than a passing fancy. Once, when Charles Smith stayed away from home too late, his father went looking for him, knowing he'd find his son at the Anderson home. Angered at his son's concept of obedience, he made his way toward the basement, but Bernadette stepped in his path. "Listen," she said, "these kids are down in this basement *doing* something. They play this stuff all night, and it drives me nuts, but at least they're trying to do something with their time. It's better than being out on the street robbing and stealing." Mr. Smith went back home.

It's not that Prince and his cohorts didn't venture out onto the streets. But when they did, they took their music with them. On Saturdays, they'd break their equipment down, bring it out of the basement, set up right there on Bernadette's lawn and jam for hours, drawing people from blocks around in the process. They'd jam until the Minneapolis police came—and they *always* came—and told the kids to take their ambitions elsewhere.

Grand Central would then move their party back into the basement and jam for hours more.

This period helped shape musical ideas and production tactics that Prince still utilizes today. Because that was all the midwest had to offer, Prince and all his musical associates in those days despised the Top-40 music they'd grown up with. Today, that attitude accounts for his penchant for releasing unorthodox singles like "When Doves Cry," a track that breaks all the rules of Top-40 by being ethereal and having esoteric lyrics sung over a rhythm track so avant-garde that it doesn't even own a bass line. (At one point in the song, the only thing there is Prince's voice and a drum machine.) Yet the song became a smash hit. There were no horns in Grand Central; Linda Anderson used to replace them with keyboard fills. It's a tactic Prince went on to use on tracks like "Head," and "Sexy Dancer," not to mention most of the tracks done by The Time.

All this local notoriety certainly improved the budding love life of the guys in the band. As Charles Smith put it, "André, Prince and I all have similar looks—the light-colored eyes and dark hair. We would have run the Jackson 5 out of town...and beat them at basketball, too!" Indeed, by most standards, Prince had blossomed into quite a looker. His huge, curly

Afro framed a handsome, well-defined face. And according to friends, in spite of his height, no one ever thought of Prince as being short. It wasn't the platform boots he wore as much as it was his confident air and sure swagger.

The band's good looks and the success of Grand Central did a lot for business down in the basement, headquarters as well for the various sexual exploits of Prince and André. Both have spoken publicly about wild times in the basement, and while it's hard to determine what is fantasy and what is reality, clearly the basement saw its share of action.

Soon, Prince and André were synonymous with more than just music in Minneapolis. Considering their good looks, it was little wonder that the two attracted their share of men as well. But they steered clear of any homosexual activity.

Surprisingly, drugs weren't a part of Prince's sexual escapades. Sure, some of his friends may have smoked marijuana, indulged in alcohol and experimented with other substances, but Prince abstained. As a child, he once got into his parents' home bar and got drunkenly sick. For Prince, the experience nipped any chances of alcoholism in the bud. As for drugs, Prince was invited to smoke weed many times but didn't like the idea of "not being in control of my mind. I didn't want anyone pulling something over on me, taking my money or something like that."

Those who really knew Prince at the time recall him through it all as not the warmest individual but a loyal friend. His cousin Charles insists that "Skipper and I did almost everything together. When he wasn't with André, he was with me. He was a good cat. I remember being in the hospital with torn ligaments and being bored stiff. The only thing I had to look forward to was Prince, who would come up to the hospital with a tape recorder. He would tape Sly and the Family Stone and Ike and Tina Turner off the television and bring it in so I could hear it. It was jamming in the hallways of the place. I would look forward to seeing his little face come through the door, with my girlfriend at the time. I even trusted him with her."

For all the musical and sexual excitement going on around him, Prince was still a lonely soul. There were girls but no real girlfriend. Grand Central had started gigging for money, and in order to stop playing Top-40 stuff so much, he started writing his own songs. Just as his father's music mirrored John, so did

Prince's songs reflect Prince. Many of them were love songs concerning imaginary relationships that lamented love gone astray. Most of his songs were, by radio standards, *long*, sometimes 10 minutes or more, with several portions to them. It is another trait still present in his music. "I Wanna Be Your Lover," one of his first hits, features a series of conventional verses before moving into an instrumental groove that could be another tune altogether. On the *Purple Rain* LP, edited from "Computer Blue" to make room for the ballad "Take Me With You," is a rambling instrumental segment that wanders away from the song's original theme.

The people surrounding Grand Central were a close-knit group. Others would try to hang out at Bernadette's basement, but the circle often proved too tight to penetrate. Anyone who did get through the barrier would most likely be brought in by someone within the circle. That is how Morris Day first met Prince. Day was one of Charles's classmates in a photography class. They became close enough that the day came when Charles felt Morris should meet his other friends. Day, a drummer just like Charles, immediately got on well with the Grand Central clan. Perhaps *too*

32

well, in Charles's eye, because ultimately Prince and André decided they wanted Day as their drummer in place of Charles. Even back then, Prince and company were heavily into politics, and Day's induction offered what seemed like advantages: Day's mother was probably as interested in her son's musical future as Bernadette was in André's work. She seemed to have connections about town, and the group was now itching to do something besides play Top-40 music.

Thus, Day's mother became a sort of manager of the group. The first major decision was to change the group's name from Grand Central to Champagne. The next move was to make some kind of demo and get themselves a recording contract. Charles was hurt by the sudden move. "I liked Morris, and the cats didn't really take to anyone so easily. I felt like Morris had come in and stolen my friends." *And* his position in the band.... It wouldn't be the last time Charles would feel Prince's hot determination to make it as a star—no matter whose feelings were at stake.

After some playing about town with their new name and drummer, Champagne booked recording time at Moon Sound, an 8-track demo studio on Minneapolis's north side. Moon

Sound was owned by Chris Moon, a young Englishman who helped comprise what little music business existed in Minneapolis. He'd promoted some local concerts for KQRS Radio in the mid '70s, establishing his name among the city's progressive music crowd. But actually, Moon was a frustrated songwriter in search of a songwriting partner. When this little funk band called Champagne came into his studio and tracked some songs, he was most impressed by its apparent leader, Prince.

It was common practice for Moon to offer local musicians free studio time if they'd write music to his lyrics. He felt Prince would make the perfect collaborator and presented a proposition: In exchange for studio time, Prince would put music to Moon's lyrics; if it turned out that they landed a hit song, the two would split all profits equally. The deal served both perfectly. Moon would turn his lyrics into songs, and Prince, eager to work in a studio, would be allowed to learn more about the technique of recording.

As their working relationship progressed, Moon discovered that Prince was able to play all of the instruments on the rhythm tracks—guitar, bass, drums and keyboards. By then he'd shown Prince how to operate the control board and was supplying Prince with lyrics, giving him the keys to the place and leaving for the evening. "He'd stay the weekend, sleep on the studio floor," Moon told *Rolling Stone* magazine. "I wrote down directions on how to operate the equipment, so he'd just follow the little chart—you know, press this button to record and this button to play back. Pretty soon, I could just sit back and do the listening."

Moon and Prince worked together like this for months, Prince showing up, always sipping a chocolate shake from the ice cream shop across the street. Moon decided that their songs needed marketability, something that would draw attention to them. Sexuality was something that always got attention, he reasoned. Why not write lyrics that have a double entendre? Using that formula, the two came up with the melodic, Top-40ish "Soft and Wet," later to be Prince's very first hit record. Moon and other musicians agree today that, more than anything Prince encountered sexually, it was Moon's suggestion that sex sells that made him run with the whole sexual image that he's created.

Prince was learning a lot in the studio, but that didn't ease the edginess that continued to eat at his creative soul. He proposed to the band that they go to New York and try to get a deal. He presented the idea to the rest of the band, but all were against it except André, who had no real immediate answer at all. Prince has said that the situation symbolized his relationship with the group almost from the very beginning. "I always felt like it was me against them. I would want to do things and they wouldn't. Nothing was happening in Minneapolis; I felt that going to New York was better than sitting around there."

Prince, who had by now obtained enough credits to graduate early from Central High, scraped up enough dough from the band's gigs to get himself a ticket to the Big Apple. Once he got there, he'd stay with Sharon, an older sister on his father's side. Friends from the period aren't sure, but they believe Sharon is the same sister who visited Minneapolis from New York. They remember Prince being very protective of her. "It was as if he didn't want anyone getting too close to her. He wouldn't let any of the guys talk to her. She was real pretty."

In the meantime, Moon, in possession of a demo tape of Prince songs, was interested in taking the situation further. However, he wanted someone who could take the tape and get a deal with it. He called Owen Husney.

Owen Husney was another of the Minneapolis music business contingent. He was a musician himself in the '60s, a guitarist with a local band. He'd worn many hats on the local music scene, working as a tour publicist for Sonny and Cher, Alice Cooper and The Rolling Stones before becoming a booking agent in the Twin Cities. He also catered the food backstage at local concerts. While backstage, arranging the bologna-and-cheese platters, Husney used to eavesdrop on the conversation of managers and entertainers, and learn. That led to Husney buying radio advertising time for acts that came into town and, ultimately, an advertising business that earned some five million dollars a year nationally. However, Husney's real interest was to work in the music business on a grand scale.

"Chris came to me and said he had 'the next Stevie Wonder,'" said Husney. "You can hear that a million times in this business, so I wasn't too enthused, but I agreed to listen." Moon showed up at Husney's office and played for him a demo of Prince songs, each of which, according to Husney, was about ten minutes long. He remembers none of the songs being especially good but still felt something distinctively special in the musicianship. "Sometimes it's not in the songs," said Husney. "That tape had nothing on it that the record companies would seriously consider, but it did have heart. The person on the tape was totally into what he was doing, and that's what caught me."

After listening to the tape, Husney turned to Moon. "The songs are not much. Kinda long. But I like the way it feels. Who is the band?" "The band is a sixteen-year-old kid named Prince," Moon answered. Husney's mouth dropped. "Whaa...Does he live in the Twin Cities? Is he signed?"

Moon and Husney concurred that with some direction and polish, this young unknown could indeed be pop music's Next Big Thing. For Husney, the opportunity to nurture such a talent meant a chance to break into the Big Time just the way he wanted, by creating something different, something special.

Husney, with his varied experience in the music business, felt he had what it took to guide someone like this young Prince to success. There was only one problem, said Moon. "Right now, at this very minute, Prince is trying to get a deal—in New York."

3.

In Search of a Dream

Prince's journey to New York is comparable to the cliché story of the country boy coming to the big city. The only person he knew in all of Manhattan was Sharon, an older half sister on his father's side. He had called her while in Minneapolis with the news of his journey east, and she urged him to come. She liked Prince and felt that he had talent. She also felt that managing her brother's fledgling career would help her make a great foray into show business.

When Prince hit the asphalt of New York, he was ready for anything. He was disgusted with the life he had left in Minneapolis. Paining him was the fact that he and André Anderson separated with a difference of opinion. He and André had grown both as musicians and virtual brothers. Prince was disappointed that André hadn't seen fit to set foot outside the Twin Cities to try to get something happening, but that's the way it was. Prince had his own mission.

Prince's sister immediately went to work trying to set up meetings with producers, record companies, and whoever else would listen. In her connecting with different people, she met a manager-type who had a band of his own. In their exchange of notes, the manager revealed that he had an appointment with a woman entrepreneur from Paris and that something might be cooking. He invited Prince's sister to go to the meeting, and she in turn, brought Prince along. At a small office in Manhattan, the Parisian entrepreneur, a woman named Danielle Mauroy, asked the manager to put his act's demo tape into the recorder. The music that came out of the speakers was pretty mundane, and the manager immediately began making excuses. Those weren't the real musicians playing on the tape, he said. As the music got worse, so did the excuses.

Prince's sister seized the moment and began telling Danielle how talented her little brother was. Danielle asked Prince to sing for her, and he refused. "Why?" she asked.

40

"Because I'm scared."

And she said, "You don't have to be afraid." They turned the lights down in the room and Prince launched into his high, frilly falsetto, singing a capella the song "Baby," which he had just written that same day and would ultimately record for his first album. Since the song was brand new, Prince really didn't have all the lyrics together and hummed his way through some parts, but Danielle loved his voice. She invited Prince to her apartment and told him to bring all of his songs.

Meanwhile, back in Minneapolis, Husney and Moon were trying desperately to catch up with Prince in New York. When Husney finally got the phone number to Prince's sister's apartment, days later, he found the musician just in the nick of time. "When I finally reached him on the phone, he was thinking about signing all his music publishing away to this lady from Paris," said Husney. "We started talking, and I tried to let him know that I was interested in what *he* wanted; I didn't see him as just a vehicle for myself. It took a couple of phone conversations to get him to consider coming back to Minneapolis."

As disgusted as Prince was when he left Minneapolis, his conversations with Husney encouraged him. Husney was saying something that nobody else had, and that was that *nobody* should produce Prince but *Prince*. It peeved him a bit that outside of his band and friends, no one really believed he could play all the instruments on his demo.

Besides, back in New York, things had begun to go bad. With no job or any income, Prince was beginning to run up a bit of a bill, and his sister wanted him to sell his music publishing for peanuts. Prince, in his ever-independent manner, felt that he could form his own publishing company. There were other disappointments. Danielle, the entrepreneur, didn't like *any* of Prince's other songs, not even "Soft and Wet." She was crazy about "Baby," but insisted that it be done with a full-blown production of horns, strings, timpani and a dramatic arrangement. Nowhere did her vast concept call for Prince to play any instruments on the track, and to him, that was a real bummer. As he has said, at that time, he didn't really care about the money; all he wanted was to see his name on an album cover, with liner notes saying he played *something*.

In the meantime, the group Champagne died a quiet death. The unit did some gigs around town after Prince split, but for the most part, it just sort of fizzled, with everyone in a holding pattern, waiting for something to happen. Prince's return was certainly a beginning. Prince immediately rekindled his friendship with André; after all, the Anderson family's basement was still home, at least for a few more weeks. The next order of business was to meet with this Husney guy. If Husney's actions were as good as his long-distance rap, Prince thought he just might be onto something.

"He was shy, but not all that shy," Husney said of his first face-to-face meeting with Prince at the home of Husney and his wife, Britt. "Moon brought him by my place one evening, and we talked further about what he wanted to do with his career. We got on real well, right from the start."

The first thing Husney did was put Prince on a $50-a-week allowance. Prince was broke, and now he'd at least have pocket change and bus fare to get to Moon's studio, where he continued to sharpen his skills. Husney then secured more instruments for him to play and something that seemed like a milestone for Prince at this point—his own apartment. It wasn't anything fancy, simply a one bedroom apartment in a complex on Lyndale and Franklin. But for Prince, it was a castle. When he wasn't at Moon Sound, you could find him at his new digs, surrounded by all of his equipment and writing songs. In fact, Husney had his share of problems with the apartment's manager—Prince was driving the other tenants crazy with this noise he called music.

Since Husney had shown his sincerity, it was now time to talk about a management contract. During this period, Husney wasn't the only person interested in handling Prince. Danielle didn't like any song but "Baby," but Prince knew she was still interested. And there was yet another possibility. According to insiders, Eddie Anderson, André's older brother, and a local Black businessman named John Jefferson were also interested in managing Prince. Jefferson supposedly went so far as to finance a trip to Los Angeles for Prince, who was in search of a deal. Reportedly, Prince was seriously considering Anderson and Jefferson, but in a zero-hour decision signed with Husney. These sources say the same thing happened again only recently, when the Minneapolis-based CBS Records act The Girls, once managed by Eddie, abruptly turned to Husney's direction. If the stories are true, then it is little wonder that, after losing two acts to Husney, Eddie Anderson is a bitter man.

44

Husney disputed the claims. "As far as I know, there was never anyone talking to Prince but me. If Eddie had something going on, that was between Eddie and Prince. I was never aware of that." In any case, Husney signed Prince to a management contract and put Prince to work at a better equipped studio—Sound '80—with a Husney associate, David Rivkin, engineering. This was an invigorating period for both Husney and Prince. Finally, Husney had found just the act he had been searching for, and Prince found someone who believed in him.

Husney claims he was the first to introduce Prince to the idea of using synthesizers. (André also claims to have been the first to make that suggestion.) "When we went into the studio, Prince wanted to record 'Baby' using horns and strings. I don't know whether he got that idea from the lady in New York or not, but I told him that he should consider using synthesizers. Both Moon and I felt that synthesizers were going to be the sound of the future, and I suggested he go in that direction. I'm not saying I showed Prince the first synthesizer he ever saw, but as far as I know, he hadn't considered using them until I brought it up."

Ultimately, Husney got Prince an Oberheim

4 Voice synthesizer, which he used to fiddle with in the studio. Synthesizers gave him even more musical independence. The demo tape consisted of two songs: "Baby" and "Soft and Wet." They recorded a third track, "Make It Through the Storm," as a backup; if Husney met with a music executive who wanted to hear more than the demo, he'd pull "Storm" from his back pocket. Once the demo was complete, Husney turned to the subject of Prince's image. He felt Prince's music was different for the times—he wanted to give him an image to match.

"The *first* thing I did was push his age back," Husney said. "Prince was pretty amazing as it was, able to play a whole rhythm section. The idea that he was young would make that point even stronger." Instead of using his full name, Husney recommended that Prince simply use his first name. Through his ad agency, he produced fifteen press kits, at a cost of $100 each. On the front of a glossy black folder was the name Prince. Inside, instead of the usual biography of the artist, there was simply a picture of Prince with one instrument and a single quote. To read on, you'd have to turn to the next page where there was another picture of the newcomer with another instrument and another quote. This went on until the last page, where Prince was pictured, surrounded by all of the instruments.

"My plan was to use an old P. T. Barnum tactic," said Husney. "I remember when I was small and the circus came to town, they'd put up signs that said, 'The Bearded Lady Is Here.' Well, once you paid your money, the bearded lady might be something else altogether. But the intrigue is what got you in there. I felt like the less Prince revealed about himself, the more the record company and ultimately the public would want to know." Thus, Husney says it was he who came up with the concept of keeping Prince a mysterious musician who people would always want to know more about.

With the demo finished, Prince's image and bio in hand, Husney knew it was time to head out to Hollywood and start knocking on doors. He had a plan for that, too. "We went into Los Angeles in suits," he said. "We wanted to be different, to stand out. If we were going to New York, we would have worn flowered shirts, because there, everyone wears suits. But in L.A., in general everyone is really casual, so we did just the opposite."

Once in Los Angeles, Husney made an appointment with Russ Thyret at Warner Bros.

Records. Thyret was a promotion man in the company whom Husney first met when he wrote some ads for a Warners' campaign a couple of years ago. Husney was considering a job at Warners at the time; Thyret was one of the few people at the company he became close with. In Thyret's office, Husney worked his technique: he let the exec first read the press kit and then played him the demo. If Thyret wanted more, Husney'd pull out "Storm." Prince would wait out in the hallway. After the kit and the music, they always wanted to meet Prince.

Thyret loved the music. He introduced the tape to others in the company and was very influential in getting the whole Prince concept over to other Warners' officials, many of whom weren't initially overly enthusiastic.

Once Husney lit the fire at Warners, he contacted several other companies, including CBS Records, A & M, and RSO, the label then flying high on the success of the Bee Gees' *Saturday Night Fever* soundtrack (which, at the time, with 24 million copies sold worldwide, was the largest-selling album in the history of the recording industry). Along the way, Husney had retained Lee Phillips as Prince's attorney. Phillips represented some of the biggest names in

48

the music business. He still represents Prince today.

Through it all, Prince was mystified. Here he was in Hollywood, filing in and out of the gold-record-lined hallways of major record companies—places he'd previously known only as logos on album jackets. It was one of the most exciting experiences in his life. "Prince was really cool during the beginning," said Husney. "He did the things I asked him to do, and our friendship was growing. We would laugh together. He had a great sense of humor. Sometimes you could look at him and tell that maybe something else was on his mind, maybe his family or something like that."

In the meantime, the relationship between Thyret, Husney and Prince was getting stronger. In the weeks to come, Thyret would drive the two around L.A. in his sports car— Prince was small enough to fit into the back— and they would all speak of the possibilities. The other labels were coming around, too. CBS voiced a passing interest, and, ultimately, so did A & M. On the other hand, Al Coury, then president of RSO, turned them down cold, as did the now-defunct ABC/Dunhill label. That was all right. Husney was most interested in signing with Warners; the other companies had cold corporate reputations, but Warners had a feeling of family/corporate warmth. Ironically, it was the company that was the hardest nut to crack.

But one day, weeks later, after Prince and Husney had retreated back to Minneapolis, they *did* crack. Warners was indeed interested in signing Prince, but with one specification—someone else produce the album. The idea of a deal was terrific. The proposal that Prince use a producer wasn't. Husney flew into L.A. to talk about it.

Warners didn't totally believe Prince could play all of the instruments on his demo, and they felt he was simply too young to produce his own first album. Instead, they suggested Maurice White, the leader/producer of Earth, Wind and Fire, then one of pop music's most successful bands. (Interestingly enough, when Michael Jackson and his brothers made one of the biggest moves in their careers—leaving Motown—CBS, their new label, suggested that White produce their debut LP there. Instead, the honors went to Philadelphia producers Kenny Gamble and Leon Huff.)

Prince hit the roof when Husney told him of Warners' suggestion and wrote Husney an in-depth note as to why White couldn't produce him. Basically he felt that White could offer nothing new. Other labels, meanwhile, were slowly changing their minds about Prince and were interested in talking. Husney flew back and forth to talk with them all. A & M offered Prince three homes in Beverly Hills for the duration of his contract as a teaser in their deal. CBS hosted expensive luncheons, at one of which the label's Earth, Wind and Fire member Verdine White was present. "Is Verdine White supposed to impress me?!" Prince huffed to Husney after the lunch meeting. "All *he* can play is *bass*!" Warners was getting closer. "At one point," said Husney, "I was at home in Minneapolis getting calls from Mo Ostin [president of Warner Bros. Records] and CBS, both offering big money. Suddenly, it was like being in a candy store." A & M sent an urgent telegram signed by company heads Herb Alpert, Jerry Moss and Gil Friesen saying the company was really interested in signing Prince, not to deal with anyone else. But it was too late. The offer Husney and Prince were waiting for finally came, and it was from Warners.

Still, they weren't home free. The company was insistent that Prince settle on a producer and wouldn't relent. Prince made several demo tapes for the company. One day they'd say yes, Prince could produce himself, the next week, no. Finally, Husney came up with an idea: Fly Prince out to Los Angeles, he told Warners, put him in the studio and have producers secretly watch him work. If they said he was good enough, he'd be allowed to produce his album. Warners agreed to the deal.

Perhaps to this day Prince doesn't know it, but when he was asked to lay down some tracks in an L.A. studio while strangers lurked about the control room, he was actually being observed by some of Warners' top producers. Assembled behind the glass that day were Ted Templeman, producer for the Doobie Bros.; Lenny Waronker, a producer who is now president of Warners' Record Division; Russ Titelman, producer who worked with Rufus and Chaka Khan; and Gary Katz, Steely Dan's producer. After Prince had laid several instrumental tracks, Waronker pulled Husney to the side and said, "We'll let him produce the album." He added, "We'll have to make our money on his second album." Apparently, Waronker didn't think Prince's first album would sell, but he was willing to take a chance on the kid's artistry anyway. Prince was already experiencing the benefits of one of the reasons

Husney had fought so hard to get him signed to the label in the first place. The company's only stipulation was that Prince's project have an executive producer, a technical hand who had experience in creating hit records. Engineer Tommy Vicari was chosen for the job.

When Prince flew back into Minneapolis, he had a feeling of exhilaration that he could hardly contain. As a team—he as the creative force, Husney as the business person, and attorney Lee Phillips as the negotiating vehicle—they'd secured for Prince a three-album deal ultimately worth one million dollars. It took them two years to do it, but Prince was now a recording artist.

4.

Fantasy Becomes Reality

There was no shortage of bitterness among the old members of Grand Central when it came to Prince. They'd all had their problems. But the news that he had finally signed a recording contract obliterated most of that. The clan and its supporters were all generally happy that he'd succeeded. Perhaps, they thought, now that one of us had made it, he will reach back and help us all.

Husney, in the meantime, invited Tony Vicari out to Minneapolis to begin work on the album. Sound '80, the studio where Prince's demo was recorded, would play host to the production, and the owner was so elated to receive a major project that he had a whole new console installed. He meant well, but recording an album on a newly installed console is a no-no in the record business. The technical kinks are not out yet. After one night of recording, Vicari simply gave up.

Moving the project back to Los Angeles was the most logical thought, but that is exactly what Husney wanted to avoid: "I did not want to go back to Los Angeles, because I thought the town would just overwhelm Prince, and I didn't need that," he said in retrospect. "Warners was depending on us to come through, and that's exactly what I wanted to do."

Nevertheless, Vicari insisted that none of Husney's protective measures would mean anything if they didn't have a professional atmosphere in which to create. Husney came up with an alternative. It would cost them a fortune, but they'd fly to Sausalito, California, and record at the Record Plant studio there. Comparatively speaking, Sausalito, although only minutes away from San Francisco, was a quiet little laid-back town that would not be so distracting. Prince loved the idea of working at the plant because two of his heroes, Sly Stone and Carlos Santana, both used the place. Husney notified Warners, and they were set.

Prince's entourage for the project consisted of Husney, his wife, Britt, Vicari, and André. They settled into a comfortable tri-level apartment overlooking San Francisco Bay and went to work.

Husney remembers Prince as a perfectionist

55

throughout that first project. "He was into it totally. He wanted everything to be just right, and he was always asking how this worked, how that worked. He wanted it all to be authentic. For instance, when he recorded 'So Blue,' he waited until he was in a melancholy mood and he had a cold."

Prince remembers the situation somewhat differently. "I'm proud of it [the album] in the sense that it's mistake-free and it's perfect," he told journalist Barbara Graustark. "But it wasn't really me, it was like a machine...I was sleepy all the time. I didn't really feel like recording for eighty percent of the record...The relationship between me and the executive producer that they assigned me was horrifying."

Just the opposite of his relationship with Vicari was his interaction with Britt. For the duration of the project, Britt took care of Prince like a mother, preparing his meals, cleaning his clothes, even combing his huge Afro. They shared enjoyable, insightful talks, and Britt turned Prince on to the music of Joni Mitchell, which Prince plays over the PA systems before his concerts today. There were some special thrills during the production. Once, during Prince's recording time of three in the afternoon to six in the morning, Sly Stone stopped by the studio; Prince also got the chance to meet Carlos Santana.

Nevertheless, some of Warners' fears had materialized. Prince did get through the album, but it took him six months to do it. The album's budget was $150,000; Prince spent $172,000. He composed, performed and produced the whole thing, but there were others involved—keyboardist Patrice Rushen, also a young musical prodigy, aided Prince with the programming of the synthesizers. And depending upon who you listen to, André contributed his musicianship to the project as well.

No matter what the circumstances, Prince had finally finished the project, and when he got back to Minneapolis, he was a hero. He had accomplished what all of his cronies dreamed about. Prince had said the experience made him a better person, and little wonder; family woes and artistic frustration over the years had made him bitter and cold. Finally succeeding at something earned him the respect of his peers, and more importantly, it gave him a special self-respect. "When Prince finally got back, it was like someone coming home from the army," remembers Charles Smith. "He played an acetate of the finished album [a prototype record; one of the very first copies of an album], and it was like angels singing. It brought tears to our eyes. Prince just sort of sat there, kinda shy-like but proud. We took him down to the basement, and when he walked in, all the equipment was set up. He went over to the piano, and without saying anything, we all just started jamming."

Of course, Prince didn't want to hear about any of it, but his work was just beginning. The first album left him over his head in debt to Warners, and the way that the company calculated it, Prince wouldn't be out of the red until three albums later. It's always hard for a new artist to get attention from the media and radio stations, and the album wasn't exactly selling like hotcakes.

Prince already knew half the game; he'd been reading *Billboard* since he started recording, and he kept badgering Husney about buying ads in the industry magazines. Warners took out some full-page ads in the tradition of the image that Husney had concocted for the press kit. There was a full page with nothing on it but the question, "Who is Prince?" and the Warner Bros. logo at the bottom of the page. The closest thing to the big time that some of Prince's partners would get would be wearing their Prince T-shirts. But there was more to be done. Like most debuting pop artists, Prince was called upon to do some promotional junkets, shaking hands and kissing babies.

The first time Prince made a public appearance was at a San Francisco record store. The album had been on the streets for several weeks and its single, "Soft and Wet," was getting some attention from local radio stations. Warners suggested that he begin his promotional work there. When Husney and Prince pulled up outside the store in their rented limousine, he was thoroughly surprised by what he saw. A line of patrons, mostly young girls, were standing outside the establishment, some of them holding Prince albums. It was the first time he had ever received any reaction to his music outside of his circle of musical associates and hometown audience; Prince was flabbergasted.

Inside the store was something else still; Prince was positioned behind the counter with pen in hand, autographing albums, casts on arms, whatever. Prince was fearful and joyous all at once. He loved the reaction to his presence, but the idea of so many people wanting a piece of him (and they all wanted to kiss him, pretty and ugly girls alike) frightened him. At one point, as the tension was building, one rather humongous young girl in line said out loud, "Yeah…he's givin' out kisses, all right, but I want *mine* in the *mouth*!" The girl looked over at Prince. Prince looked sheepishly at Husney. Husney looked away, trying to hold back his laughter.

There was plenty of that kind of mingling to be done. Special appearances in clubs… Visiting radio stations and meeting with disc jockeys, hoping that his presence would entice them to play his record…Socializing with music business types at promotional parties. Prince didn't really seem to mind. He'd dance with the women and receive pompous compliments from people who had never even taken his record out of its jacket. Months of this apparently paid off. In 1978, "Soft and Wet" became a national hit record, moving up the Black music charts. The success of the single helped Prince's album, but not much; it only sold about 100,000 copies. Warners had by no means even begun to recoup its investment, but even those meager sales figures gave them hope.

However, after all that time in the studio and, the series of personal appearances, Prince was beginning to feel more like a foreign diplomat than a musician. Everything he had had emerged from the concept of the live band, and he wanted to get back to that. Husney secured a warehouse for him, and Prince began auditioning musicians for a touring unit. Once again, things were changing in Prince's life. He'd moved into his first home, a nicely furnished place at 5215 France. Just as he settled into his new home, he was also settling into music business politics. Before, he simply sat back and listened to what Warners and Husney had to say about things. But more and more, he was beginning to ask questions about the business aspects of his career. In any case, he felt that now was the time to hit the road.

Once the word got out that Prince was putting a band together, local musicians seemed to smell their way to the warehouse auditions like bloodhounds. Prince already had the pulse of his rhythm section together; André would play bass guitar and Charles Smith, aced out of Champagne when Morris Day joined the group, was back on drums. Prince told Smith he could play if he found the band a keyboard player; Smith corraled a girl named Gale Chapman. In a matter of weeks, the rhythm section saw many a musician come through that warehouse. There was Sue Ann, a young vocalist who would later record an album of her own under Prince's direction; Cynthia Johnson, who would ultimately sing lead for Lipps, Inc., on a disco smash called "Funky Town." There was Rockie Robbins, a comparatively conventional soul vocalist who would record his own albums for A & M Records.

Weeks later, after an army had paraded through the warehouse, Prince settled on his new band. In addition to the other members, he added Dez Dickerson, an articulate young rock guitarist who answered an ad Prince put in a local newspaper, and Lisa Coleman, a classically trained pianist who would replace Chapman as keyboardist.

One night after a rehearsal session, all of the equipment at the warehouse was stolen. Whether Prince accidentally left the door unlocked or whether thieves forced their way into the place is still up for debate among local musicians and hangers-on, but whoever came through after rehearsal cleaned the place out. "What happened was, we were all sitting around at Prince's place when a girl called and asked had we left town and come back already," Charles Smith recalled. "Everyone in town knew about Prince going on tour. We told her that we hadn't gone anywhere, and that's when she told us that she had seen someone moving instruments out of the place. We all piled into somebody's car and flew over there. Everything was gone."

The major thing that makes the incident noteworthy is how it affected Prince. He was starkly silent as he looked over the empty warehouse, occasionally cursing the burglars under his breath. Some who remember the scene have implied that the door may have even been left open on purpose; inevitably some band members felt that they were given the once-over as possible culprits. In any case, Husney reported the theft to Warners, and eventually they sent new equipment.

But before the equipment came, Smith noticed what he deemed a change in Prince's demeanor. With everyone looking to him for the new instruments, Prince was clearly in control. And he seemed to relish it. "Folks were asking about the equipment every day because it took so long for them to send it," he said. "Prince would get mad if you asked too many times." When the new equipment did come, it all legally belonged to Prince. According to Smith, Prince seemed to come across a case of amnesia when it came to his drum set. "I never got my set back. Weeks went by, and I'd call, trying to catch him. Sometimes he'd tell me to come by his house at a certain time, but he wouldn't be there."

A drum set is not all that Smith lost. Another drummer named Bobby Z. had been hanging around the rehearsals; his impromptu sitting in with the band led to a permanent position in Prince's new group. Once again, Smith had been edged out of the band. Still, even that didn't hurt as much as what Smith says was his last real communication with Prince. "It became pretty obvious that I wasn't going to get my drum set back," he said. "I started picking up some gigs around town, so I asked Prince if I could *borrow* his set for a while, especially since mine had been stolen from the warehouse." According to Smith, Prince looked at him and replied that he didn't have to do anything for him, that he was now a star.

Other musicians of the period who refused to allow their names to be used ("Hey, you never can tell...I might be in one of the bands that Prince pulls out of here and decides to produce," said one musician) agree that they saw a change in Prince. "He never was Mr. Personality, but to me, he seemed to change when the Warners deal came through. In fact, I'd say he stopped hanging around Black people all together when he made that record."

Others have indicated that Prince was advised to racially integrate the band so he'd have a better chance of mass acceptance. In any case, his very first tour was as the opening act for Motown artist, Rick James.

When Prince and his band hit the stage, most of James's audience would spend the first few minutes of the set merely gazing in bewilderment. They seemed genuinely alienated by Prince's preoccupation with long, intense guitar solos and onstage rock'n'roll attitude. Plus they didn't care for this guy's decidedly feminine gestures, like the constant flinging of his straightened, shoulder-length hair out of his eyes and those bikinis he made a point of stripping down to. But when he'd break into one of those relentless grooves, like "Sexy Dancer," he usually had the crowd rocking in the aisles.

Whether Rick James will ever admit it or not, he had to be an admirer of Prince. After all, it was easy to see that, like James, Prince had a vision. It wasn't long ago, but as recently as 1980, when Prince hit the scene, that Black audiences in general weren't totally ready for the musical melange Prince was offering. It was easy to see what Prince was after: *everybody*—whites, Blacks, anyone looking for musical freedom. Though James's sound was easier to categorize as R & B, James prided himself (as he still does) on molding the live energy of rock with the definitive pleasure of modern funk.

Regardless, he'd be one of the first professional musicians to get a whiff of the Prince enigma. In rock, it's not uncommon for opening and headlining acts to become rivals. Rock music abounds with a zillion stories of professional jealousy, of one act outdoing the other, of technical sabotage, of fights over dressing rooms. According to those close to the situation, James's anxiety about Prince began when Prince refused to be social. Rick made several attempts to break the ice common among opening and headlining acts, but Prince and his entourage wouldn't respond, performing their set and retreating to their own after-hours intermingling. "It didn't help matters that Prince's set was absolutely smoking every night," said one observer on hand for the stand-off. "People weren't crazy about some of that shit Prince would play, but when he got funky, sometimes he'd have them climbing the walls. Nobody wants to come after something like that; it makes you work too damn hard."

According to the same source, the straw that broke the camel's back came when, after a live set, Prince refused James's mother an auto-graph. "He just walked away...turned his back on her," said the observer. "Rick didn't dig that at all." Whether any of those incidents were the reasons for it, James went on an anti-Prince campaign, telling the national press of his con-tempt for Mr. Minneapolis. Among James's charges have been that Prince's music is a bad influence on today's youth, and that Prince's girl group, Vanity 6, was taken directly from James's Mary Jane Girls, which was a concept that he had formed earlier.

Prince, in his typical nonchalant fashion, has never once acknowledged James's statements, though it is believed that musical entertain-ment wasn't what was on his mind when he attended Rick James's 1983 concert at the Uni-versal Amphitheatre in Los Angeles. When Prince made his entrance, escorted by his bodyguard, Chick, just before the lights went down, the place nearly succumbed to pande-monium, with women shrieking and even Mo-town executives getting on their feet to get a glance at Your Royal Baddness. Prince got to his seat but not ten minutes later, rode piggy-back on Chick out to the concession stand and then later, repeated the gesture during the in-termission between the Mary Jane Girls' and

James's sets. The crowd loved it. When his entourage returned, the house was waiting for it, and the audience spotted Prince even in the dark, as Chick carried him out, cradling him just like a baby, just before James hit the stage. Prince had royally upstaged Slick Rick's act without singing a single note. (Prince showed a considerably higher level of respect at a Jacksons' Victory Tour date in Dallas, intently observing Michael Jackson's fancy footwork from the sound booth.) Backstage, James, informed of Prince's little charade, was unmoved: "I'm not bothered by that; Princess obviously came to learn from a pro."

A physical and musical hybrid of Jimi Hendrix and Sly
Stone, Prince is still one of rock's most original performers.
(Paul Natkin/Star File)

Prince as he entered Mann's Chinese Theatre to view his first movie, *Purple Rain*. *(Gary Leonard)*

Like some of the best rockers, Prince has mastered his own trademark scream. Here he gives his lungs a workout. *(Bob Leafe)*

The mesh of reporters and fans outside Mann's Chinese Theatre awaiting the arrival of guests for the *Purple Rain* premier. *(Gary Leonard)*

A rare off-stage photo of Prince between two music industry executives. At the far right is the infamous Chick, Prince's bodyguard. *(Gary Leonard)*

One of Prince's biggest onstage assets is his uncanny ability to fuse musical imagination with heated passion.
(Paul Natkin/Star File)

Apollonia Kotero *(right)* greets Prince band member Jill at the *Purple Rain* premier bash. *(Wayne Byrd/Way-Mat Photos)*

Morris Day, clowning for camera and interviewer at the *Purple Rain* party. *(Wayne Byrd/Way-Mat Photos)*

The Time's original lineup. *From left:* Terry Lewis, Jimmy Jam, Morris Day, Jellybean Johnson, Monte Moir and Jesse Johnson. *(Photo courtesy of Howard Bloom Agency)*

Vanity 6, the original version of Prince's girl group. Vanity *(center)* is flanked by Brenda *(left)* and Susan. Vanity left the group and was replaced by Apollonia.
(Photo courtesy of Warner Brothers)

Prince takes center stage during 1983's record-grossing 1999 tour. *(Bob Leafe)*

Prince during his bikini and leg-warmer days, circa the 1981 album *Dirty Mind*. *(Bob Leafe)*

"Mr. Minneapolis" sporting a flashy
(Paul Natkin/Star File)

version of his famous trench coat.
(Paul Natkin/Star File)

Guitarist Dez Dickerson at the *Purple Rain* party. Dickerson left the security of Prince's band for a solo career.
(Wayne Byrd/Way-Mat Photos)

André Cymone, Prince's childhood friend, who left Prince's fold for a solo deal and the chance to spread his wings.
(Randee St. Nicholas. Photo courtesy of Columbia Records)

During live shows supporting his *Dirty Mind* LP, Prince established the trench coat as his fashion trademark.
(Bob Leafe)

Prince onstage during his Controversy tour. In the background are guitarists Marc Brown and Dez Dickerson.
(Bob Leafe)

When Prince is onstage, he leans on his audience for participation, and they usually respond enthusiastically.
(Paul Natkin/Star File)

5.

Managing the Unmanageable

Prince's second album was a lot easier to make. By now, after the response from his first album and debut national tour, he had a better idea of what the public wanted. He was also better skilled at making his music. Though Warners' Artist & Repertoire department kept a close eye on his progress, the developing artist was allowed to produce his second album. This time Prince, with Husney and André, went into Los Angeles to record. The result, an album simply entitled *Prince*, showcased the work of a more refined artist, perfecting what would become a trademark of his—melodic pop tunes countered by strong rock and funk overtones.

"I Wanna Be Your Lover," the first single from the LP, was the epitome of the style dominating Prince's writing in those days—bright, catchy verses equipped with a mind-imprinting chorus. Move into the album version of the song, though, and you find a streamlined, synthesized lyricless groove, accented with Prince's funky rhythm guitar strokes. The only thing smoother than Prince's vocal delivery here is the track's danceability. The fact that his biggest hits are also dance-floor gems accounts for much of Prince's mass appeal, but this is often overlooked when critics analyze Prince's dramatic crossover strength.

"I'm certain that it's at least one reason for his huge success," Husney has said. "I mean, yesterday, it was serious rock; today, it's happy feet. They're all trying to do it, from Mick Jagger on down. But nobody fuses the two better than Prince."

Prince hit the jackpot, literally, selling beyond gold status (500,000 copies sold) but stopping just short of the one million mark. The record was a huge success in that it put him on the map among professionals. Today, after *Purple Rain*, the whole world knows of Prince, but even by the second album, Prince's far more successful peers were already predicting that he was a kid to watch.

More importantly, *Prince* demonstrated to Warners once and for all that this guy from Minneapolis was a bankable entity, indeed.

What the Warners people *didn't* like, however, was what looked to be growing internal conflict between Prince and his manager. With a couple of hits under his belt, Prince was now understandably confident, but Husney noticed that his client was, on occasion, downright cocky. It seems by nature that the artist—whether writer, painter, actor or musician—can be one of the most insecure species on the planet. Self-assuredness is often simply a generator that keeps these people going. But increasingly, Prince was questioning Husney's game plan.

The most immediate problem was that Prince was steadfastly refusing to do any more promotional work. He didn't want to do any more interviews and visits to radio stations because these people didn't understand him and often misinterpreted what he said. Warners was looking to Husney to straighten things out, but he was having problems doing it.

In the meantime, there were some promotional chores that even Prince didn't mind tending to, at least once anyway. As a kid, he'd seen his share of *American Bandstand* episodes. Along with the success of "I Wanna Be Your Lover," came the opportunity to play the show. After his lip-sync performance, Prince never really ever spoke, but shook his head for yes and no in response to Clark's questions. At one point, when Clark asked how long he had been making music, Prince would only use his fingers to express the amount of years. Clark, visibly irritated, cordially gave up and let them get to the next number. Insiders joked that Prince had just blown his one ticket to ever appear on the show again. Little did they know the artist would outgrow the medium of television altogether.

It was episodes like that T.V. taping that Warners would ask Husney to straighten out. In turn, Husney told Prince how important it was that he cooperate with the company, that they were all in this together, but eventually Husney's pleas would only bounce off Prince's brick wall of silence. It was clear that their association was deteriorating. Today, it's hard to pinpoint exactly what went wrong; Husney will not discuss the situation on the grounds that it is "highly personal." But others say Prince simply did not think Husney was capable of taking his career to the heights he envisioned.

"I don't believe Prince could actually have thought *that*," Husney refuted. "I was the one who got him one of the best lawyers in the business and fought with Warners to get the creative freedom he now enjoys."

Prince hasn't offered much more insight on the split, albeit he has acknowledged that he was stubborn and bullheaded regarding the issue of promotion. Nevertheless, according to insiders, Prince was later angered that he had to pay Husney a hefty amount to get out of his management contract with him. "I made money with Prince, I'll admit," Husney replied, while not directly addressing the speculation. "But looking back on those days, handling Prince gives Moon, my wife...it gives us *all* credibility. *We* were the ones who took a chance on Prince. Everyone else has simply inherited what we helped build."

That still doesn't stop Husney, whose American Artists Management firm now handles André Cymone, The Girls, and ex-Time guitarist Jesse Johnson, from pondering the outcome had the chips fallen differently. "I *do* wonder what [would have happened] if all this had happened for André first," he said. "After all, they both put the whole thing together, I really do wonder sometimes."

Around the latter part of 1980, André must have been wondering that very same thing. Like Husney, André was also having his share of problems with Prince; their disagreements were becoming more intense. André has maintained all along that it was *he* and Prince who were the pulse of Prince's musical creativity, and that their working together had always been a natural process. But just after the release of the *Prince* album, their differences intensified.

For instance, when Prince appeared on *American Bandstand*, André wore a pair of bikini briefs. After the taping was finished, he was asked not to wear them anymore, but later during future performances, it was Prince who would come out in the bikinis. "I should have known something was up then," said André.

What bothered André most, however, was disturbing evidence suggesting that Prince really felt that his band only had room for one creative head—his. In interviews, André, despite what all the publicity says, insists that he contributed musically to Prince's albums but received no credit or money. Indeed, only recently did André receive a framed gold-record plaque for the *Prince* LP, which, according to local hangers-on, is an admission that André had something to do with the project after all.

"That groove on the end of 'I Wanna Be Your Lover' was actually just something

Prince's band used to play at jams at the warehouse before rehearsals," said one musician. "When people heard it on his album, everyone knew where it came from." Another from the Minneapolis music community claimed that for a while, not many musicians wanted to play with Prince. "Let's put it this way," the source said, "Prince always had the tape recorder going in rehearsals. He recorded every note anyone played."

Prince was aware of the stories being whispered about him by the locals, but finding new management after Husney was the biggest task facing him at the moment.

Management is a vital part of an entertainer's career. If the act is lucky, it links up with someone who is both artistically perceptive, to offer creative direction, and able to negotiate away any roadblocks in the path of the act's creativity. In Prince's case, the mission was to find someone who, first of all, could deal with *him*. At this stage in his career, it was especially vital that he have representation.

Of course, there is always a manager willing to take on a promising act, but those courageous souls who attempted to take on Prince found it was Mission Impossible from the outset. There was Perry Jones, an L.A. music-biz type, who lasted for a hot minute. And there was Don Taylor, who had previously worked with Bob Marley. "I just wasn't the man for the job," Taylor wearily admitted back in 1981. "This guy was just too weird for me. I never knew *where* he was coming from. He'd start recording at one studio, and if something went wrong, he'd want to just scrap the project and book time someplace else." However, even back then, Taylor somehow knew the truth: "Whoever is able to deal with that boy will make a million dollars," he said, shaking his head.

As it turned out, the job took *three* men, Bob Cavallo, Joe Ruffalo and Steve Fargnoli, known to millions of readers of album cover liner notes (and now movie credits) as Cavallo, Ruffalo and Fargnoli. Cavallo and Ruffalo, the main partners in the company, were already managing Earth, Wind and Fire, Weather Report and Ray Parker, Jr., when they signed Prince at the urging of Fargnoli. In the span of just three years, Prince and his satellite acts have overshadowed anything the management team has ever been involved with.

C, R & F inherited Prince just as he was to deliver his third album to Warners, and their managerial capabilities were immediately put to the test. "It was a mess," said one former employee of the firm. "Prince was used to doing things his way, and they had to let him know that things could get done if they all worked as a team. Once he saw that they could really help him, everything was just fine."

In fact, it was Prince's management company that would encourage him to move ahead with the album project that would forever alter his career and set him on the road to superstardom once and for all.

6.

Prince: Minneapolis's Music Machine

Who knows where Prince would be today if his third album had turned out as Warners and, reluctantly, even he had originally planned it. Maybe he'd be playing some glitzy lounge in Las Vegas or gaining notoriety as some saccharin pop music maker. Or just bubbling under anything innovative or musically significant, forever confined to plastic half-hour pop music T.V. shows. Actually, Prince was already bored with what he'd created. He was happy with success but he looked upon his last two albums as lackluster. It didn't take him very long to grow weary of singing "Soft and Wet." Today, the song isn't even in his set.

To alleviate this musical monotony, Prince would, like many musicians, make his own demo tapes, musical ideas apart from what he presented to the public, just for his own ears.

One day he played the tapes for Fargnoli, to get his reaction to the songs. He figured Fargnoli's reaction would be negative, but perhaps some of the songs could augment his third album. The sparsely produced tape featured rough versions of the songs "Dirty Mind," "Sexuality" and a thing called "Head," an explicit tale about a bride-to-be and her last fling on the way to the altar. To Prince's surprise, Fargnoli loved what he heard. "This should be your album," he told Prince.

The executives at Warners didn't see it that way. These songs featured explicit lyrics about wanton sex in the backseats of cars and a generally renegade view of life. It was a long way, they reasoned, from the G-rated direction of the singles "Soft and Wet" and "I Wanna Be Your Lover." As it was, there wasn't even one such song on this tape. "I thought *Dirty Mind* was an album that deserved to be made," Fargnoli told the Los Angeles *Times*. "But Warner Bros., understandably, didn't know how to react. Prince's last record had sold almost a million, and they expected something with the same sound. They were very negative about the music at first."

The company gasped once again when they saw Prince's idea for the album cover. There he was, his now infamous trench coat open, looking much more menacing than the gentle boy on his first two covers. You followed the body hair down his bare chest...on past his stomach to...those black bikini briefs! The back cover wasn't much better, showing Prince stretched out on a bed in lewd splendor, his legwarmer-clad legs crossed. Warners got nervous all over again. It was bad enough that the music went out on a creative limb, but this cover could even scare away the potential customers in droves.

Fargnoli, however, stuck to his guns. Nothing could be changed, he insisted. It would ruin the whole concept. Ultimately Warners relented; they had another idea. They'd label the front of each album jacket with a warning that the contents on the inside were definitely not for the weak or the timid. Sales of *Dirty Mind*, released in 1981, fell considerably behind the almost-platinum status (one million copies sold) of its predecessor, *Prince*, and with good reason: except for the uptempo single "Uptown," almost none of the LP could be played on the radio, forfeiting valuable exposure. But the album more than made up for its immediate sales in that it established Prince as he wanted audiences to accept him—a swaggering free spirit with the reins to do whatever he damn well pleased. "I wanted to go beyond the audience that would just come to your shows only when you had a hit record," Prince reasoned. "I wanted to develop a following that would see me as me, and not just some guy with a Top-10 record."

With that in mind, Prince again hit the live circuit, this time not as an opening act for anyone but headlining small clubs, like the old Flipper's skating disco in Hollywood. In his usual outrageous garb, Prince, with André, Dez, Lisa, Bobby Z and Dr. Fink, a new addition on synthesizers, rocked the place silly. This concert has made rock history as one of the city's most memorable. The tour wasn't technically or financially groundbreaking; Prince was still a virtual unknown to mainstream audiences. But it was this series of impassioned, electrifying performances that suggested to national critics that Prince was someone to be reckoned with.

Meanwhile, back at the ranch—specifically, Prince's new home on Lake Minnetonka—it was business as usual. Prince's pad served as a sort of hangout for musician friends and band members, though he was never one to completely share his private abode. Home was a retreat from the often hectic music business, and he used the solitude to create virtually miles of music. When other artists are filling sides of their singles with old material, Prince can still afford to fill his B sides with new songs. Relative loneliness has allowed him to generate a glut of material.

Some people couldn't understand Prince's introspective ways. He seemed abnormally clandestine at times, especially when it came to talking about his family. "The more successful he became the more guarded he was about his personal life," said a musician who shared a mutual friend with Prince and visited the artist's home several times. "If a conversation came up where folks started talking about their families or whatever, Prince would clam up. He seemed to be kinda paranoid sometimes, too." Others recalled that even though Prince never gave the impression of being greedy, he certainly recognized the fact that money meant *control*. Even though Prince by now had plenty of money in the bank, one source has said he hides cash in shoe boxes at his home.

Prince's quiet time was usually divided between his music and romance. Romance? Perhaps sexual companionships is a more appropriate term. There was never any *one* woman in Prince's life back then. They just sort of came and went. While the public and the press pondered his sexuality (Prince further fueled the fire by toying with the question of his sexual preferences in both the songs "Uptown" and "Controversy"), those who really knew Prince simply laughed at the accusations. "Sometimes, we used to lie there in bed, and he would ask me what I'd heard about him, you know...sexually," said one young Minnesota beauty who claims to have known Prince in a special way during the period. Unlike Apollonia, who staves off queries of any Prince romance with the response, "I don't kiss and tell," this former flame wears her claims of Princely intimacy like an Olympic medal.

"He was interested in knowing what people thought about him. He would ask me, 'You ever hear anybody saying I'm a fag?' The thing that got me was that he wasn't doing anything to make people think that he *wasn't* gay. He'd wear eye-liner and earrings. If you didn't know him, you'd have thought that he *wanted* people to think that. But looking at the way he's led his life since then, I'd say that he just dressed the way that he wanted to. He really didn't *care* what people thought."

And if you were one of Prince's women, caring was an art. No matter how you felt about Prince, you'd have to control your feelings, because Prince always had women at his beck and call. According to this past companion, to Prince, a one-woman relationship seemed like some vivid fantasy more than anything else. "I think a one-on-one relationship is something he'd like very much, but he won't let himself go. But the thing that makes him so attractive to women—other than his looks—is how he treats women. Even though he always has more than one female interest, he treats them all as if they were the only one."

In 1981, however, romance in Prince's life took a backseat to music. Not only did he use the year to present his adventurous new musical direction, but it was also the year Prince decided to utilize his musical insight beyond his own act. Before *Dirty Mind* was accepted by Warners, Prince had been toying around with other grooves, some R-&-B-based things he figured would comprise his third album. Now that the *Dirty Mind* concept was a reality, he wanted to further develop those other tracks. Thus, the idea for his first protégé band, The Time, was born.

Like anything Prince gets involved in, the

creation of The Time was not without its share of controversy. According to André Anderson, who by then was using the surname of Cymone, The Time was a project that he and Prince were supposed to nurture together. André has claimed that it was he who came up with the concept, that he was going to write and produce the project, but that Prince took over.

Jesse Johnson, guitarist for The Time, remembered the forming of the group somewhat differently. He was raised in Rock Island, Illinois, by white foster parents. Before embracing The Time's slick, cool image, Johnson played rock 'n' roll guitar in a Rock Island biker dive. He ventured into Minneapolis at the suggestion of a friend who told him that he reminded him of this guy there named Prince. Morris Day, who was playing drums in a band called The Enterprise after Champagne had fizzled, was one of the first friends Johnson made there.

"I was just sort of feeling the place out, trying to fit in. I stayed in both [Time bassist] Terry Lewis's attic and another friend's basement," he said. (Where would musicianship in Minneapolis be without basements?) "Morris came by one day and said he might have this gig for me. He said he and Prince were gonna put together a band and it was gonna be real big. He thought I might fit in. The cats in The Enterprise thought he was crazy, but it sounded good to me." A couple of days later, Day brought Prince down to Johnson's basement and introduced the two. "He was real nice," Johnson recalled. "He came in, we shook hands, and he told me he'd heard a lot about me from Morris. We talked for a little while. I thought he was going to ask me to play guitar, but he just kinda looked me up and down, turned to Morris and said, 'Yeah, he's got it.'"

Having secured the band's guitar player, Prince then recruited bassist Terry Lewis, keyboardist Jimmy Jam, Monte Moir and Jellybean Johnson from a local band called Flyte-Tyme. In the early days, FlyteTyme was one of the bands that gave Grand Central/Champagne the most competitive heat. It was ironic that years later Prince would raid the band for its core. Depending on how you choose to look at it, Prince either stole the unit's best members, or as one onlooker viewed it, "He went in there, kicked out Alexander [FlyteTyme's lead singer] and put Morris Day in." Nevertheless, The Time was now complete, just in time to attend a photo session for the band's debut Warner Bros. album, simply entitled *The Time*.

Who actually played on the first Time album is questionable. In his usual show-biz fashion, Prince concocted a tale of how he discovered the band playing in a local Minneapolis bar, but the truth is, a record deal for The Time as a group had been consummated before any of the executives at Warners even saw the band. It has been said that the first album was performed almost totally by Prince, that he sang the leads, then had Day come in and follow them to the letter, ultimately mixing his own voice out. Though the liner notes credited Morris as the composer of the album's songs, it is known that Prince is registered at ASCAP (the American Society of Composers, Authors & Publishers) music licensing organization as writer of at least "Get It Up" and "Cool," and his music publishing firm, Controversy Music, administers the songs. A Jamie Starr is listed as the album's producer, but a couple of years ago journalists exposed the fact that the name was actually a pseudonym for Prince. He now produces albums other than his own under the banner of the Starr Company.

In listening to Time tracks like "Cool," "Get It Up," and "The Stick," you can certainly hear

Prince's pipes supplying background vocals and his distinctive rhythm guitar work. "I'd love to tell you who played on that first album, but I don't know," Johnson conceded. "I've heard that everyone from Prince to Lisa [Coleman] all worked on it."

No matter who performed on the record, it became a hit, with the album going gold and the band itself emerging as one of the tightest, most enjoyable live R & B/funk units in pop music. The concept was brilliant: five dapper, impeccably dressed young men supplying stylishly synthesizer-laden funk for lead vocalist Day's onstage exploits as a dashing, annoyingly egotistical, jet-set ladies' man. Day was joined onstage by his loyal valet, Jerome Benton, who took the occupation of Yes Man to new heights with his mid-show onstage pampering of Day with everything from a mirror and a comb to a table for two, champagne and a female guest plucked from the audience for Day to share it with.

This spectacle is the closest any new band has come to combining music and vaudeville stage antics since the old, show-stopping revue days of soul greats Joe Tex, and Ike and Tina Turner. The success of The Time, however, marked the unofficial end of the musical relationship of Prince and André Cymone. Cymone said he simply grew weary of doing everything Prince's way, contributing to his projects for no money or credit. Prince asked Cymone to stay with the band and offered him a raise of two thousand dollars a month. "But I wanted the *whole* band to get a raise," André said. "Here Prince was living in his second house, and I was still at the pad with my mother. I added too much to his thing to be treated like that."

Instead, Cymone signed a management deal with Owen Husney, Prince's original manager, who in 1983 secured him a solo contract with Columbia Records. His two solo albums, *Living in the New Wave* and *Survivin' in the '80s* both died early deaths. He produced one side of R & B singer Evelyn King's 1984 RCA album *Shakedown*, which was only a marginal success, and he produced the debut album of protégé girl group, The Girls. As of this writing, Cymone is working on a third solo album.

In the wake of André's split from Prince, more than one peer has asked, If André was influential to Prince's musical development, why has his own career faltered so? "I think that André is just trying to do something totally different," Husney surmised. "Anyone coming out of Minneapolis is going to be overshadowed by Prince—simple as that. André sees it as a challenge. But what we're going to have to do is start at the beginning, with a great dance record. That seems to be all Columbia Records understands Black people doing, so we're going to give it to them. Then we'll work our way to what André wants to do."

"I have no ill feelings for Prince," André said in retrospect. "I've gotten over my bitterness, and I'll always think of him as a brother. I have nothing to hide; that's why *I* do interviews. He [Prince] has come by the studio to listen to my work and that sort of thing. It's not like we don't speak. I believe that we'll work together again—producing something, maybe, when the time is right. But I spent a lot of time investing in someone else's thing. Now I have to get mine."

7.

The Ascension

The most invigorating thing about Prince is his unpredictability. *Dirty Mind* had left no doubt that he was going all the way with his sex-is-freedom crusade. After the success of The Time's debut album, the world wondered how its producer could possibly compete with it, since The Time, with its more R & B sound, found its audience so quickly. But later (1981) when Prince's *Controversy* album was released, the songs showed that sex wasn't the only subject that intrigued Prince.

The title track itself was a handful for the Moral Majority. A dynamic march of a dance vamp, it has lyrics that seem to deal with everything on Prince's mind at the moment—his mild annoyance with queries about his sexual preferences and whether he was Black or white. But the most poignant gesture in the song was

Prince's recital of The Lord's Prayer. Just the fact that it came from *Prince* seemed reason enough to suspect hidden, ill meanings. Across the country, some radio stations initially considered banning the tune, but the legion of callers requesting to hear just what the stink was all about forced even those radio stations to play edited versions of the record.

Prince wasn't toying around with the moral consciousness of America just for the hell of it; apparently, in his seclusion, away from women and song, the guy had actually been checking out the five o'clock evening news and had some views on the situation. "Ronnie, Talk to Russia," also on the album, was a public plea to the President of the United States to deal head on with the issue of nuclear weapons. During the eerie "Annie Christian," Prince painted a haunting picture of America's gun control—or the lack of it.

Maybe this influx of politics was exactly what the doctor ordered—*Controversy* became Prince's first platinum album. Oddly enough, for all his constantly budding success—both commercial, with the first two albums, and artistic, with the *Dirty Mind* project, or on *Controversy*, which marked the combination of both—Prince was still something of a stranger

108

to most pop audiences. His singles got ample air play on Black radio stations, some on pop stations, but little on rock radio. Prince's management and record company fought ardently to change the rock radio situation, but Prince still refused to do the obvious peddling of his wares, like press interviews and, God forbid, any television appearances.

Prince was virtually a self-made rock star. But he took the occupation one step further by creating whole bands in his own image. While The Time's concept decidedly represented Prince's more worldly R-&-B-based tastes (Stacy Adams shoes, stylish suits, jewelry, big cars, hip cats, etc.), Vanity 6 was a materialization of his dream of sexy, straightforward women who looked a man in the eye and told him exactly what was on their minds—preferably sex. Vanity 6, a sexual '80's girl group trio headed by a Canadian beauty named Vanity, who was flanked by first-name-only cooers Brenda and Susan, was big on camisoles, pin-up poses and marginal vocal talent, but who could resist something as hypnotically danceable as "Nasty Girl," the trio's lewd-lyriced first single?

Vanity, a.k.a. D. D. Winters, had worked as a model in her native Ontario and even had a couple of B-movies under her belt—*Terror Train* and *Tanya's Island*, a Robinson Crusoe-ish flick that has since been relegated to cable T.V. heaven—when she met Prince backstage after one of his concerts in 1981. She introduced herself as a songwriter, but Prince didn't hear that as much as he noticed her distinctive looks—penetrating brown eyes, long, dark hair framing a classically beautiful face, and those legs.

Prince suddenly found the perfect idea for another act. *Vanity 6*, the act's debut album, also on Warners, featured funk with an edge, with songs like "Drive Me Wild" and the raucous monologue of "If a Girl Answers (Don't Hang Up)." The group's first album produced by the Starr Company scored well in 1982, selling almost 500,000 copies. However, Prince had scored much more than just another hit record. He and Vanity immediately became an item. For months they did everything together, and Vanity moved into his Minneapolis home. Prince even stopped seeing his harem of other women, which his friends took as an indication that he was somehow becoming emotionally stable.

"When we saw Vanity's face around Minneapolis more than just three times, we said,

'Oh shit! The Kid is acting like he's in *love*,'" said a fellow musician. "It's not Prince's way to tell too many people how he feels about a chick, and he didn't say anything to me, but just that they were spending a lot of time together meant something. Prince is not the kind of cat who lets too many people, man or beast, in his personal life for very long. She'd already made a coup in that respect."

Living in Prince space, however, meant eating, drinking, living Prince. "Despite his free-thinking spirit, those acquainted with Prince during the period still knew him to be pretty conventional when it came to his treatment of lovers. If he wanted to be with the fellas in the band, he was with the fellas in the band; the chick stayed at home or found something else to do—if he considered whatever else she decided to do was cool with him. Control is a big word in this man's life, so you can imagine what he expects of his girlfriend." Apparently, though, it takes more than simply donning an apron to please Prince. An observer close to the situation recalled some tough times between Minneapolis's new couple.

"Prince is a wonderful person—let me get that out right now," said the observer, another of Prince's ex-lovers. "But he's a genius, and geniuses are intense. The way he was with Apollonia in the *Purple Rain* movie—you know, that scene where he asks Apollonia to jump in that lake and then gets mad because when she gets on the back of his motorcycle, her wet clothes drip on the seat—that's the way Prince really is. I understand one night he and Vanity had a disagreement while they were driving home from a movie. He pulled the car over to the curb and said, 'You can *walk* home.' I think that she ended up taking a cab that night. But here's a man who isn't a wimp. Believe me, Prince is *all* man."

Others weren't as generous in their observations of Prince. Some people thought he was downright weird. Somewhere along the way— perhaps it was the "Controversy" single—an increasing number of people were wondering if Prince had more than just musical genius on his side. Locals liked to talk about whether or not Prince was a student of the occult. They attributed the possibility of it to Prince's strange and secretive ways. Even Owen Husney had a thought on the subject. "Well, you think about the fact that this guy doesn't do interviews, makes these explicit records and still comes out on top. It's almost as if he made a pact with the man downstairs."

Husney made the statement jokingly, but a photographer, who lived in Minnesota briefly while on business, said that when he met Prince, he looked into the artist's eyes and "felt like someone was going through my pockets. I'm scared of him."

"Oh, I'm so tired of hearing all that shit," said a former employee of Prince's who insisted, "I've spent enough time with him to know. I never saw Prince doing any hocus pocus when I was around; I think he would have tried to turn me on to it. The problem with Minneapolis is that everyone in the town is either in awe of the guy or jealous of him. There are people here who will never go anywhere, and they like to pull people down. If Prince is into devil worship, then I'm having a serious affair with a Gumby doll."

Apollonia has related the story of her first meeting with Prince, at an audition for her co-starring role in *Purple Rain*. "The first question he asked me was, 'Do you believe in God?' I told him 'Of course.' He said, 'Good.' I know he's aware of where his talent comes from."

Then there are others still who believe that Prince is obsessed with the idea that he is some great savior to the people around him. Many of his songs, these people point out, contain lyrics that suggest Prince is an omnipresent being. To support their claim, they turn to a line in Prince's "I Wanna Be Your Lover," where he, in a caressing falsetto says that he wants to be not only the woman's lover, but also her mother, brother and sister.

"Prince always thanks God on the back of his album covers," said one observer. "Yeah, but the word G-o-d could mean *anything*. Your God could be a tree in the woods," said another, and so the controversy continues.

Not even Prince realized just how naturally making music came to him until he started pondering his next album. Life was good these days, and he was sporting all of the luxuries of a rich man—he had moved into a gaudy, two-story home on the secluded outskirts of Minneapolis, painted, of course, Prince's trademark color: purple. The few visitors who found their way into the place report that it was sparsely furnished with items that could only be described as, well...*different*. "It's somewhere between what a hippie and royalty would have at home," said a visitor to the place. "Let's put it this way—it ain't conventional. Unless he's gotten rid of it, one room is filled with nothing but fan mail. Bags and bags of it. You'd be surprised what people send him.

I've seen panties in some of the large envelopes. Sometimes he'd go in there and read the mail when he was really bored." There is also a big black BMW automobile, a new limousine, a purple custom tour bus and a purple Honda motorcycle, which now has been seen by millions in the movie *Purple Rain*.

Interrupting Prince's calm, however, was what he and management deemed a very special invitation. The Rolling Stones were on their 1981 world tour, a series of concert dates that was one of the biggest, most expensive tours in the history of rock music. The Stones had been calling on a series of good but underexposed acts to open national dates—George Thorogood and the Destroyers was just one of the acts whose status was lifted by massive exposure from opening for what has been called the "World's Greatest Rock 'n' Roll Band"— and they called on Prince to open for them during their Los Angeles concert at the Memorial Coliseum.

Warners and management had already pulled all stops in their quest to have Prince accepted by rock radio. An opening slot with the Stones would further validate Prince to rock radio program directors as an artist for all people, and, they hoped, he'd come away from the Coliseum with some new fans as well.

What could have been a very lucrative experience turned into an absolute disaster. Almost immediately after Prince and his band hit the stage, almost 100,000 people started booing, hurling paper cups, fruit and obscenities toward the stage. A local radio station was broadcasting the concert live, and you could even hear the sentiment of one ticket-holder shouting in the background, "Get that faggot off the stage! Bring on the Stones!"

Initially, Prince and company simply kept on playing. He'd experienced his share of hecklers as a child with Grand Central. Back then, there were a couple of instances involving Black patrons who didn't want to hear what they deemed to be white rock 'n' roll from a band with Blacks in it. Unlike those situations, the difficulty at the Coliseum was that the more he played, the louder and more aggressive this crowd became. They wanted him *out of there*! Not even ten minutes into the set, Prince stopped playing and left the stage. "I left because I didn't feel like making music anymore, I felt like *fighting*. I wish I could have gotten my hands on a couple of those guys down near the front. I had twenty minutes up there, and they wouldn't let me finish that."

The irony of this situation was the fact that just prior to Prince hitting the stage, this crowd had sat contentedly listening to tunes blaring over the PA system, tunes by Jimi Hendrix, a (Black) rock giant who made history with his uncanny ability to move masses of all colors and who is the artist to whom Prince is most often compared. Quite frankly, this was a Rolling Stones crowd, interested in seeing nobody but the Stones and it probably would have booed Santa Claus. (The J. Geils Band, on another date opening for the Stones, was also booed.)

An associate at the Cavallo, Ruffalo and Fargnoli office mentioned that Prince was "pretty depressed after the Stones date. Who wouldn't be? Booed off the stage? That's pretty bad. He didn't want to come *near* L.A. for a while." But Prince did come back, months later, and delivered a nonstop, action-packed, headline show at the Santa Monica Civic Auditorium, a show so hot it nearly burned the place down. His energy on stage was relentless! "Good thing this place is just a few blocks from the Pacific Ocean," said one fan out in the lobby after the set. "We won't have to run so far to get water."

* * *

After the Controversy tour, Prince spent most of his time sequestered in his truest pride and joy: a fully equipped 24-track home recording studio. Inside, Prince kept at his fingertips state-of-the-art synthesizers, electronic drums and an arsenal of guitars. This is where Prince spent a lot of his time in 1981 and 1982, simply laying down rhythm tracks, exploring his various musical whims. "He always used to say, 'Man, when I get some cash, I'm gonna have my *own* studio,'" Husney said. "In the very beginning he was always scraping around borrowing this and that. I think that he made up his mind that one day he wasn't going to go through that number again."

Prince is always working on another album; that is, he is always recording *something*. When the time comes to gather material for a project, he simply chooses what he likes from a selection of songs he's already recorded, and he may write newer ones to supplement what he's chosen. There are always new songs; Prince is always writing.

That is how *1999* was created. It featured songs that Prince had recorded over a long period of time. Some of the songs were two years old; some of them came to him just months before the album was to be released.

118

"[Prince] went to his managers, and they came to us," said a Warner Bros. executive, who didn't want his name mentioned because "I don't think he's crazy about people on his team discussing him with the press. But they came to us and said, 'Look, Prince has got all these songs that he just wants out there. He's written so much that he's ended up with enough music for a two-record set. That's what he wants to do."

Depending upon who you confer with, Warners either loved the idea or simply shook in their corporate boots. On one hand, Prince was due for another roll of the dice. His career had been that from the very beginning. His records, despite their controversial subject matters, were consistent sellers. The projects he'd presented to the company, The Time and Vanity 6, had both done extremely well for debuting acts. The only chance left for Warner Bros. to take was releasing a double record set of Prince material that might not sell. (Record companies have shied away from releasing double albums in the last few years, because consumers have been resisting their higher price tags.) Warners, on considering Prince's past, was willing to take the risk.

The company found some measure of security in the album's first single, a tune called "1999." Aside from all the usual ingredients found in successful Prince singles—immeasurable danceability and an unforgettable lyric hook—the people at Warners especially liked the fact that there was something that this Prince record *didn't* have—obscenity. In fact, "1999" was the most uncontroversial single to be released by Prince since "I Wanna Be Your Lover," unless you consider a song about a person dancing his way through Armageddon controversial. The Warners people were banking that the record would give Prince the kind of rock radio exposure he had never had but always wanted. Their optimism was understandable, but they refused to examine the fact that the album *1999* was *chugged* with what Prince does best, which is, anything he wants to.

On one of the project's four sides of wax, Prince put the First Amendment guarantee of freedom of speech to the test with "Let's Pretend We're Married." In that number Prince vividly described everything he wanted to do with a mate as they feigned matrimony. The hot dance anthem "D.M.S.R. (Dance Music Sex Romance)," encouraged festive carnal/musical anarchy, while the white heat of the torch bal-

120

lad "International Lover" used a clever double entendre of sex and a plane flight.

It's interesting; it seems like the bigger the career risks Prince has taken, the more magnificent the gain. That crap shoot called *Dirty Mind* made it possible for Prince to take the gamble of *1999*. Thus, it stood to reason that a double album's-worth of artistic risks could only generate an incredible commercial and artistic jackpot. And that is exactly what happened.

Released in 1982, *1999* took the nation by storm. There were three Top-10 singles from the album—its title track, the modern synthesized rockabilly "Delirious" and the inventive "Little Red Corvette." The success of the album spawned the 1999 tour, which extended into 1983. It was during that historic tour that audiences got the chance to see Prince's empire in its prime: most of the shows across the country were opened by the sexy Vanity 6. Their short set made way for the snazzy R & B of the mighty Time, only to be followed by the creator of it all. When Prince took the platform amidst a whirl of multicolored smoke by sliding down from the stage's second level on a fireman's pole, he reminded many people of Elvis Presley in the movie *Jail-*

house Rock. When he squeezed a string-bending solo out of his electric guitar, he brought back images of the unforgettable Jimi Hendrix. When Prince broke into one of his show-stopping dance routines, complete with spins, turns and splits, one was forced to conjure thoughts of Little Richard in his rock 'n' roll prime or the Godfather of Soul, James Brown. Indeed, Prince was everything an entertainer is supposed to be: *Entertaining*.

By the time the smoke cleared, Prince's *1999* album had sold almost four million copies. It was a collection of songs that audiences had paid almost ten million dollars to see him perform live, setting a 1983 tour-grossing record. Prince as a producer, songwriter, musician and entertainer had indeed arrived. But the world hadn't seen anything yet.

8.

Trouble in Paradise

Nineteen eighty-three may have proven to be a banner year for Prince, with the *1999* album and tour expanding his audience immeasurably. Even while that victory was being won, Prince was preparing for an even more devastating assault on the entertainment world. No one really knew what Prince spent his nights on the tour bus scribbling into a purple notebook during the band's crosscountry trek. But the attention that he gave that notebook suggested that he was working on something big indeed. Soon enough, the word was out: Prince wanted to make a movie.

Prince had introduced some strange ideas to management in the past, but this one posed a special challenge because, for the first time, both Prince and his managers would be operating like fish out of water. C, R & F, like anyone who did anything successful in Hollywood, often thought of making movies, but the hope was usually a cliché one for anyone in the music business. It was "that next step" that every artist worth his gold records wanted to take. However, the closest that many of even the most successful artists ever get is talking about it to journalists in interviews or portraying themselves on some television show. Prince wanted to make a movie, but he didn't feel that he had to wait until he sold a zillion records; for the moment, Michael Jackson and his *Thriller* LP that was selling so phenomenally had that situation well under control, but even he hadn't attempted to make a film based on his own ideas. After weighing the possibilities, the management team agreed; they'd make a movie. The concept would emanate from Prince's head. Raising the money and working out the specifics of the project would be handled by the management team. With the decision made, the ambitious project went into development.

In the meantime, however, Prince had some serious matters to deal with immediately. Internal problems were developing in his musical empire. In the beginning, with the release of their first album, members of The Time were content to have a record on the national charts. However, by their second national tour, augmenting the 1999 dates, the unit's members had learned a lot.

One of the things that they learned real fast was that they were primarily the musical vehicle for Prince and, to a lesser degree, lead vocalist Morris Day. That would have been fine for a group of musicians whose talents were only marginal, but The Time was comprised of some of the most proficient players in Minneapolis. Keyboardist Jimmy Jam and bassist Terry Lewis, two of the most integral members of the unit, were particularly interested in more. They'd already written some songs for the Vanity 6 project and had some good material ready for The Time's second album. Extending their songwriting skills, even doing some outside production, would make their experience in The Time the more invigorating, they thought.

Jam and Lewis went to Los Angeles looking for anyone interested in songs and immediately got responses. The Minneapolis music scene was one of the most exciting things to happen to pop music in a while, and everyone wanted to be a part of it. Jam and Lewis ended up writing and producing a track for Klymaxx, a band whose major distinction was being solely comprised of females and that was recording for the Solar label. "Wild Girl," a dynamic track composed (and actually performed in the studio) by Jam and Lewis started getting air play. That is when their problems began.

"When we got back to Minneapolis, word trickled down through management channels that someone wasn't too pleased with our working outside The Time," Jam told Lee Bailey of *Radioscope*, a nationally syndicated radio program. "It wasn't the group itself," Jam recalled. "Actually, they were real supportive of us. Morris told us, 'Man, I really like the stuff you guys are doing.' While we were recording the second LP [*What Time Is It*], things felt a little tense." To Jam and Lewis, it was soon clear. The disapproval was coming from the top; not the band, not the management, but Prince. "It was a thing of 'We should all stay together and be family,'" said Lewis. The two were requested to fly from L.A. to Minneapolis, where they had a tense meeting with Prince. During that meeting, Jam and Lewis were given their walking papers. Not long after, the two were asked to come back into the fold, but as Jam said, "At first it was felt that we weren't acting in the band's best interest. By the time they got around to asking us back, we didn't feel that The Time was in *our* best interest." Instead, Jam and Lewis packed their bags, headed for Los Angeles, and from a west side apartment, began taking on a series of projects. Since then they have become one of the hottest R & B production teams around, having written and/or produced hits for Gladys Knight and the Pips, the S.O.S. Band and Cheryl Lynn, among others. Jam and Lewis, and keyboardist Monte Moir, who left The Time shortly after Jam and Lewis, have formed a band of their own called The Secrets, and in a genuine twist of fate, produced a solo album for Alexander, the former lead FlyteTyme vocalist who found himself out of a gig when The Time was formed.

There were other complications for Prince as well. Dez Dickerson, Prince's fiery guitar player who'd been with him from the very first tour, departed from the band for a solo career. (As of this writing, Dickerson and his band were playing hard rock 'n' roll in small clubs while negotiating a record deal.) Dickerson acknowledged that Prince was the kind of employer "...you had to have an understanding with. Prince and I had a good relationship in the band because I knew from the beginning that it was his baby. I've always wanted my own band anyway; Prince was just a detour for me— a job. But I *do* think I helped push Prince in a more rock direction, which is where he wanted to go in the first place. The key to Prince is getting his respect. If he doesn't respect you, you can forget it. He respected me."

Prince's musical empire seemed to be crumbling as fast as it was built. The departure of Jam and Lewis from The Time was one thing, but now with Cymone and Dickerson gone (Cymone was replaced by Marc Brown), the Minneapolis music community agreed that Prince was in trouble. "There will never be another band like Prince's first group," said a member of Shalamar, a Los Angeles-based pop act. "We [musicians] all looked at that band as being something special. No offense to anyone, but he'll never be the same."

Dickerson, who went on to appear very briefly in *Purple Rain*, defended Prince's new aggregation to come: "The truth is, today Prince doesn't *need* the same kind of band he had when he started out. Back then, he needed a power band, people who could get him to another level. Now that he's there, he can relax a little."

No matter what Dickerson's sentiments were, Prince could do anything but relax. He turned his attention to finding new Time replacements for Jam, Lewis and Moir and came up with Terry Hubbard, Paul Peterson and Mark Cardenas. Not only did the trio step into an already popular band, they'd be in Prince's movie as well. Next, he filled Dickerson's slot with Wendy Melvoin, a guitarist and childhood friend of keyboardist Coleman. The public consensus seemed to suggest that Melvoin wasn't half the musician that Dickerson was, but as far as Prince was concerned, that wasn't the point. The idea was not to *replace* Dickerson but to make The Revolution a different band. A female guitar player would certainly get attention and it looked...hip. Prince knew that if he took his band on the road, the *real* guitar playing would have to rest solely on his shoulders, but that, too, was a part of the new concept. Now, more than ever, Prince would be the star of this show.

Meanwhile, Bob Cavallo and Joe Ruffalo had just about secured financing for the movie project, but there was no script. "Prince may have been a musical genius," commented that ex-C, R & F employee, "but there was no way they were seriously going to look to Prince to actually write a script—that would have been a *real* joke."

That was not as big a joke as the idea of

Prince starring in his own movie was to Hollywood's motion picture people. Finding someone at a major studio to take the whole Prince concept was a tough cookie to swallow for a team whose act was pop music's golden boy. In Hollywood, there are two types of people—movie people and music people. Each contingent generally looks down at the other. The movie people see the music business as a bunch of classless, drugged-out, New Age hippies who keep the business hours of Dracula. The music people view the movie folk as name-dropping, medallion-clad, cigar-smoking snobs who think that they own the town because Paramount pictures was in existence long before Motown. The fact is, until recently there has been a gap between the two industries wide enough in which to play the Super Bowl. "Prince who?...naw, we're not interested. Now if this kid of yours wants to do the soundtrack for the next John Travolta flick then we might have something..."

William Blinn was a beginning, at least. Blinn was a screen writer whose credits included the T.V. movie *Brian's Song* and a segment of the award-winning *Roots* miniseries, and who was holding down the executive producer post for the T.V. series *Fame*. Since it was up in the air

at the time whether or not *Fame* would be re-
newed for a third season, Blinn figured it wise
to meet with the Prince people and hear what
they had to offer.

Over a series of meetings with management,
Blinn was told of the proposed story, one of
a kid rocker who wants to be a star. Cavallo
and Ruffalo even had Blinn flown out to
Minneapolis to meet with Prince and discuss
his ideas for the script. Perhaps the word "discuss" is not quite appropriate; Blinn recalled
that Prince wasn't too talkative, that he basically had to listen to what the band had to say
and then recite it all back to Prince to make
sure that they were on the same wave length.

Blinn then began writing a screenplay that
was considerably more than the story ultimately shot. In Blinn's story, Prince's father
kills both himself and his wife. However, just
as Blinn's script was shaping up, he was called
back to the *Fame* production, which left Prince
and the company approximately right back
where they started. Ultimately Bob Cavallo had
a breakfast meeting with Al Magnoli, a film
editor who had recently worked on a movie
entitled *Reckless*. Over eggs and coffee, Cavallo
leveled with Magnoli—he and his camp really
didn't know *what* they were doing, but perhaps

Magnoli could steer them in the right direction. Magnoli offered some suggestions but really began to inject helpful changes when the rough draft was left behind.

The crowning touch to Magnoli's injections would come once he actually met the star himself; Cavallo flew Magnoli into Minneapolis, and this time Prince clicked with someone from Hollywood. Magnoli told the musician of his draft, and Prince liked what he heard. Prince in turn introduced Magnoli to the rest of the film's tentative cast—Morris Day and The Time, Susan, Brenda and the surrounding entourage.

In the meantime, the relationship between Prince and Vanity had deteriorated to the point where it was unclear whether or not Vanity would be in the picture—or in Vanity 6. Vanity has been mum on the subject, but it is believed that Vanity's past may have helped bring about the split.

Out of all the Minneapolis clan, it was Vanity who had the most experience as a professional. She'd modeled and played in a couple of movies; she was signed to the prestigious William Morris Agency even before she met Prince. So, when the idea of the movie came around, Vanity wanted to negotiate the situation on a very professional level, or, as the surrounding whispers implied of the stalemate, "She wanted some real money. Vanity realized that if the movie was decent, it could do well at the box office, and she wanted to make it worth her while. Prince didn't see it that way, though. The rest of the gang was just as happy to see themselves in the dailies; he was taken aback by her going for the gold, so to speak."

Not long after, Vanity had gone the way of Jam and Lewis. She moved out of Prince's purple house and moved into an apartment in Los Angeles. Her William Morris agent immediately began making calls on her behalf. There were rumors. *Rolling Stone* magazine wrote in their "Random Notes" column that Vanity would star in a film directed by Martin Scorsese. There was a rumor that Vanity would be the new member of the pop trio Shalamar ("Dead Giveaway," "Dancin' in the Sheets"), which had lost two of its members. In any case, Vanity was seen hanging out with the group's leader Howard Hewett, and its newly inducted member, Micki Free. When Vanity walked into a Hollywood premiere for a celeb-filled screening of Michael Jackson's *Thriller* video, she was on the arm of her ex-boyfriend's buddy, Eddie Murphy. That was an item for the rumor mills, but then it really wasn't an issue anymore. Vanity was on her own. Ultimately, she signed to co-star in a Motown film production called *The Last Dragon*, and it led to Vanity signing a recording contract with Motown Records as well. She co-wrote and co-produced her debut album, *Wild Animal*, for the label, and she purred and moaned her way through the project's first single, "Pretty Mess," which has lyrics that are as nasty as anything Prince ever produced. Another Prince protégé was on her way.

Prince, making his way past reporters at the *Purple Rain*
premier. As usual, he had no comment.
(Steve Granitz/Celebrity Photo)

In this scene from *Purple Rain*, Prince quietly psychs himself up for the night's gig.
(Courtesy of Water Productions, Inc., and Warner Bros. Inc.)

Apollonia and Prince embark on a fast and furious romance in *Purple Rain* that is quickly put to the test by Prince's violent mood swings. *(Courtesy of Water Productions, Inc., and Warner Bros. Inc.)*

If nothing else, *Purple Rain* allows those who have never
been to a Prince concert to experience his dynamic onstage
antics and intensity.
(Courtesy of Water Productions, Inc., and Warner Bros. Inc.)

In *Purple Rain*, Apollonia gets a chance to show off her voice as well as her beauty.
(Courtesy of Water Productions, Inc., and Warner Bros. Inc.)

Jerome Benton *(left)* and Morris Day add comic relief to *Purple Rain* and nearly steal some scenes from Prince in the process. *(Courtesy of Water Productions, Inc., and Warner Bros. Inc.)*

By his *1999* album, it was clear that Prince would one day sit on top of the world. *(Courtesy of Howard Bloom Agency)*

Reclusive offstage, Prince turns into an extroverted
dynamo in front of an audience. *(Paul Natkin/Star File)*

Prince seems to put a spell on his audience. He's been known to have the same effect on his band and advisors.
(Bob Leafe)

There's no telling when Prince, a master of onstage sexuality, might start undressing in the middle of the set.
(Bob Leafe)

"For a while, I just made music as a hobby," Prince has said. "Now I look on it as art. All I have to do is be true to myself." *(Bob Leafe)*

Though he stands only 5'3", Prince has become a giant in the tumultuous world of pop music. *(Paul Natkin/Star File)*

Not all of Prince's audiences have been appreciative; he was booed off the stage while opening for The Rolling Stones in 1981. *(Chuck Pulin/Star File)*

Critics say Prince has it all: he writes, sings, plays his music and is an exciting performer. *(Paul Natkin/Star File)*

Prince's look alters with each stage of his career. In 1979 he wore his hair shoulder length. *(Gary Leonard)*

Prince in his very first Los Angeles show, at Hollywood's Roxy Theatre in 1979. *(Gary Leonard)*

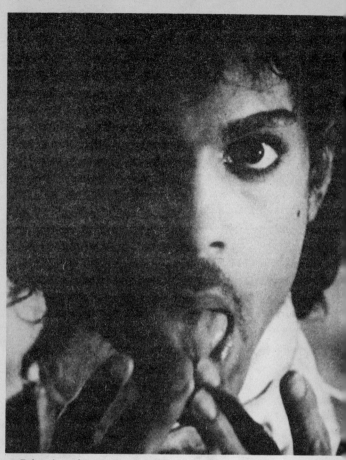

Prince's androgynous sexuality is both provocative and controversial. *(Courtesy Water Productions, Inc., and Warner Bros. Inc.)*

9.

The Kid: On Screen and on the Town

Making *Purple Rain* was *no* party. Produced on a turtleneck-tight budget of seven million dollars—measly by Hollywood standards— it was shot in the winter of 1983, right there where the "semibiographical" story took place, in and around Minneapolis. For Magnoli, there were elements that he considered to be mild handicaps—like the fact that except for co-star Patty "Apollonia" Kotero, who had worked as a model and appeared in producer David Wolper's T.V. miniseries *Mystic Warrior*, the rest of the cast were not actors. They were simply extending their true personalities to the camera. These musicians were basically famil-iar with the story line of two bands competing for top honors in a small town, with "The Kid," Prince's character, having to deal with rival musicianship and his emotions.

Revolution guitarist Wendy Melvoin has indicated that Prince's on-screen behavior toward his band is very much true-to-life, particularly concerning his lack of interest in using music that they've composed. Wendy's sentiments are in reference to the fact that Prince has only recently allowed members of the band to get involved with studio projects. On the *Purple Rain* album, not only were many of the songs—excluding the important hit "When Doves Cry"—recorded with the whole band, but Lisa and Wendy were also allowed to contribute to some arrangements. The ultimate gift was Prince allowing The Revolution's hypnotic "17 Days" to be on side B of the single "When Doves Cry." The single sold 400,000 copies in the first week of its release; at last, Prince's band shared in writers' royalties from a composition.

"It's not really any big deal that the band is getting the opportunity to do more writing," ex-Prince sideman Dickerson said. "He made it pretty clear, at least to me, that not too much writing would be done by his band until he got to a certain point in his career. I think he's reaching that stage right now."

As for the making of *Purple Rain*, the behind-the-scenes reports were far more interesting than those from Magnoli. Apollonia has told the press that when she and Prince did the love scenes "it was sometimes hard to stop." And some who were on the set aren't sure that they did.

Apollonia, an exotic Latin beauty, who may or may not be Prince's main squeeze, paints a different picture than most of Prince. In her interviews on behalf of the film, Apollonia has revealed Prince as a fun-loving, outgoing, humble, God-fearing man. "I'd heard a little about Prince before I went to Minneapolis to audition for the movie role, but I didn't go there to judge anything. I'm not in awe of him, so we get along just fine."

Perhaps Prince is lightening his iron hand of control on those around him. A couple of years ago it wouldn't have been out of the question for him to insist on Apollonia living in Minneapolis with the rest of his organization. As it is, he flies her back and forth from Los Angeles to Minneapolis.

It's been said that despite Morris Day's on-stage bravado, Day didn't want to play the role that he was stuck with. "I'm capable of better," he told one confidant. "Black people don't necessarily act like this."

Day's discontent with his role in *Purple Rain*

was just another incident in a series of Prince/ Day confrontations. The problems were apparent on the 1999 tour in 1983 before the filming of *Purple Rain*. But, even to comprehend that situation, one must go back to the infant stages of The Time.

"Prince taught us a lot about performing," said The Time's Jesse Johnson. "He used to tell me how to move with my guitar. He'd say things like, 'Now come up flashing those eyes …you've got great eyes. Use them.'" In the early days, Johnson not Day was the one always arguing with Prince over little nuances, but whatever Prince told Johnson to do usually turned out right. "I remember insisting on wearing what *I* wanted to wear onstage," Johnson said. "I was clashing with The Time's look, but I didn't care. After about a week of trying to get me to wear this certain suit, Prince gave up and went to Steve Fargnoli. The two of them cornered me. Prince just stood there listening to Fargnoli talk to me, to no avail, when he said, 'Listen, Jesse…just wear this suit. Do it for me. I guarantee you that when Morris introduces you, the crowd is gonna go crazy. *Trust* me.' That night, when Morris introduced me, they were screaming like crazy. Prince was right."

Prince was unselfish in his nurturing of The Time and often complimented the group on their outstanding opening performances. "Sometimes," said Jimmy Jam, "he'd come in after the show and say, 'Man, did you guys kick my ass *to-night*!'" Despite Prince's nurturing of and compliments to The Time, it has been said that Prince and Morris Day had conflicts in almost every city during the 1999 tour, a ritual that ended with Prince insisting that The Time not open for his shows in Los Angeles and New York.

Even before principal shooting of *Purple Rain* was finished, it was clear that Prince and Day would soon be going their separate ways. "At the wrap party for the movie, Morris and Prince didn't say two words to each other," said an attendee, "and that was real unusual for them. It was easy to see that something was up."

Between conflicts with Day, Prince was nurturing yet another stablemate. Sheila Escovedo, a multi-talented musician from Oakland, California, left a percussionist post with Lionel Ritchie's road band to join Prince's musical clan. Several months later, Escovedo had streaked her hair, settled for an initial instead of a last name and even dressed like Prince. Actually, it is surprising that Escovedo hasn't been inducted into The Revolution outright. Onstage with Ritchie, Sheila proved that she was a great percussionist, holding her own on drums as well as fooling around with the electric bass, not to mention the fact that she is not the worst break dancer.

Prince has said that he communicates more naturally with women and that there seems to be something about him—beyond looks—that attracts them to him as well. Prince's sex appeal seems to know no boundaries. His love scenes with Apollonia in *Purple Rain* have been called some of the most passionate, most convincing moments between a man and a woman on celluloid. Prince's "Kid" has been compared to Marlon Brando's Stanley Kowalski in *A Streetcar Named Desire*. Kid and Apollonia's relationship was just as tempestuous as Stanley and Stella's. Both men's raw sexuality had hypnotic effects on their women. Prince exudes the kind of animal chemistry and unadulterated passion that turns on women of all ages. It's little wonder then, that after an industry screening for *Purple Rain*, Olivia Newton-John was heard to expound on the young superstar's desireability while her beau listened on in amazement.

Jesse Johnson pointed out that the Prince who appeals to one individual may not be the same personality another is exposed to. "Prince and I used to argue—I mean *argue*," Johnson said. "I never was afraid that I was going to be thrown out of The Time or anything like that. What we had disagreements about would have nothing to do with my musicianship. He was able to separate things like that."

Comments from LaToya Jackson tend to support the view that Prince is a man of many faces: "Prince is probably a real nice person behind that mysterious image." LaToya met Prince a long time ago during his early years in show business. "He was almost painfully shy," she said. "He told me that he once had a real crush on me, and he wanted to go out on a date." But sometime later, the enigma reared its head. "Once I was with my family in a restaurant in Los Angeles and Prince was there. He saw us all there, but he and his people just walked right by and never said a word."

Though he can be reserved and introverted, Prince can easily turn on a warm and outgoing persona as well. "I think there are several different people in there," ex-manager Owen Husney said of Prince. "Prince is not always the private, secretive person that the press always makes him out to be. That's just one side of him. That is why he plays all the instruments so convincingly. See, it's one thing to merely record the different instruments. But when Prince is recording the guitar track, that's another personality playing. When he lays down the keyboards, he has still another attitude, and on and on. That's what gives his tracks passion. I've had to deal with every one of those personalities at one time or another."

When Prince steps out on the town, his many personalities are on public display. He doesn't simply go to one place and stay there. If you are in his entourage, don't make yourself too comfortable; you'll be leaving shortly.

Carlos 'n' Charlie's is a Mexican restaurant on the Sunset Strip. Above it, up the stairs, is the El Privado room, a private disco and bar, which hosts an intriguing game of Hollywood psychology: if you're a popular enough celebrity, you can walk right through the door. If you're a ravishingly beautiful woman, come in and make yourself at home. If you have money and power, you have access. Everyone else pays. The philosophy here is that the celebs draw the women, and the beautiful women attract the paying male customers. There is also another crowd, the spectators, who pay to come and watch the celebs mingle with the women.

One night after dinner at Le Dome, a posh restaurant just minutes away from El Privado, Prince and his ever-present bodyguard, Chick, made their way into the club. He and his small entourage of band members didn't walk in but *eased* into the place, like cool ghosts. With Chick not even a full step behind him, Prince made his way past the small dance floor, on past the V.I.P. railing, and found his usual seat, back in the mirrored corner. He just sat there and gazed at the people. In the past, he would enter the club and send someone up to the d.j.'s booth with a cassette of some new jam that he'd recorded and try it out on this pseudo-chic crowd, but this night, he just looked. He studied the women and who they talked to. He even examined the way a couple shook it up on the dance floor.

Suddenly, the d.j. reached back in his stash and came up with James Brown's "Bodyheat." The "heat" hit Prince's body; he wanted to dance. He slowly rose—so did Chick—and moved toward a Eurasian beauty with long dark hair who had been looking at Prince with incredible curiosity. Prince grabbed her by the hand and took her out on the dance floor. Prince put his left hand up, just in front of his chest; his right hand seemed to caress his thigh. With his feet apart just the right distance he began to rock to the groove. It was a cool sway, not much movement, but it had *passion*. The groove was killing the speakers. Prince was rocking. The crowd was watching. Prince looked at Chick; Chick gave a gathering look of his eyes to the entourage. Prince simply walked away; he was outta there.

10.

Baby, I'm a Star

July 1984. As he sat among Warner executives in an advance company screening of what would be his career's crowning glory thus far, Prince was also pondering one of his most significant conflicts—the heat between him and Morris Day. *Ice Cream Castles*, the third Time album, released in June 1984, had the potential of outselling previous Time records (*The Time, What Time Is It*), which were gold albums. However, by the time the album hit the streets, The Time as a group was all but over.

Day's growing frustration seemed to mark the end of an era. Already gone from the Prince stable were André Cymone, Dez Dickerson, Jimmy Jam, Terry Lewis, and even Vanity— a move that really caught onlookers by surprise. But somehow, Day's dissatisfaction and the threatened future of The Time seemed

161

more serious than when childhood buddy Cymone left Prince's fold. Perhaps it was because The Time was a group that, like his own band, Prince helped mold in his own musical image. Some say he molded the group in more than its music aspects. There was even a rumor that Prince marched some members of The Time into a local Minneapolis barber shop, had the place closed down and told the barber how to cut their hair. Is it simply coincidence that all the members of The Revolution wear their hair hanging in one eye, à la Prince?

If Prince marks the direction in which '80's rock 'n' roll will travel, then The Time definitely charted the path of modern funk. "The Time was a fun band," reminisced former member Jesse Johnson. "The music and the show were always about having a good time." By the end of 1983, however, The Time was no longer a band enjoying itself. After the departure of Jam and Lewis, Day told Johnson he'd give the new line-up a chance, but if it didn't work naturally, he wouldn't push it. "The thing about it was, the new band was very good," said Johnson. "But when Jam and Lewis left, it was like snatching the heart out of a person. It just wasn't the same. Morris, Jellybean and I felt like we were onstage by ourselves."

The last time that Morris Day made an appearance representing The Time was at the Hollywood premiere of *Purple Rain* in July 1984. There, he posed, gave profiles and cracked jokes. The event marked the end of the group. In reality, Day had already moved from Minneapolis to a condo in Santa Monica, the breezy, tropical Los Angeles suburb by the ocean. "Why pay taxes to a town that won't support you?" he told *Billboard* magazine. "They never played our [The Time's] records." Changing management was another professional alteration the singer/songwriter/drummer made, severing ties with Cavallo, Ruffalo and Fargnoli. "I never felt comfortable with them," Day said in retrospect. Throughout their handling of The Time, Day had never signed a contract with the management company. After the early success of *Purple Rain*, the firm stepped up their actions to get Day to sign, but he left and signed with Sandy Gallin, who also manages Dolly Parton. As of this writing, Day was working on forming and recording his new band. Jesse Johnson, who left The Time after Day, signed with Owen Husney and recorded a debut A & M solo album, *Let's Have Some Fun*, released in September 1984.

Terry Hubbard, The Time's replacement

for bassist Terry Lewis, also left The Time and joined Johnson's band.

Day will pursue an acting career as well as music, and both he and Johnson have projected that their respective new groups will fill the void left by the original Time. Day wants The Time to be remembered as "one of the fastest rising R & B bands around in a long time. Bands like that don't happen everyday." True. However, The Time was doomed from the very beginning, eventually suffocated by something most bands can't get enough of: too much talent.

However, out of the old comes the new. Time drummer Jellybean Johnson, keyboardists Paul Peterson and Mark Cardenas, and ex-Day valet Jerome Benton comprise yet another new Prince band, called The Family. They, Sheila E. along with Mazaratti, a band discovered by Revolution bassist Marc Brown, form yet a new generation of Prince protégé acts.

When the movie *Purple Rain* was finally completed in 1984, Warner Bros. Pictures, which had finally—but not without reluctance—gotten involved, first intended to book the film into a grand total of six major theaters across the country. The fact that Prince and his roster of acts had so much success at its pany, Warner Bros. Records, obligated the company to at least distribute the film, since they wouldn't initially get involved in financing. Then they invited film and rock critics to screenings. Not only did sneak previews in San Diego and Denver sell out, but film and rock critics were immediately entranced. *Rolling Stone* magazine called the movie "the smartest rock 'n' roll movie ever made." *Newsweek* suggested that Prince be anointed as the screen's "newest and most singular idol." Weighty kudos perhaps, but during *Purple Rain* Prince did it all. He bridged that gap between rock music and drama in a unique way and did a splendid job of presenting rock performances on celluloid. The advance praise was enough to make Warners open the flick in more than seven hundred theaters nationwide.

Not surprisingly, *Purple Rain* was a multimedia triumph. The movie's soundtrack album sold more than two million copies in its first couple of weeks of release. Two videos from *Purple Rain* were among the most popular videos on both MTV and local TV shows. In just one week, the movie had grossed $7.7 million dollars, just a little more than the project had cost to make.

Though Prince and his contingent started

working on the project right after the 1999 tour, the artist couldn't have planned a better strategy for the summer of 1984 if he'd employed advisors from the Pentagon. During a season when the blockbuster tours of the Jacksons and Bruce Springsteen dominated the year's live rock business, *Purple Rain* was the perfect bargain. For about five dollars a ticket you could be entertained by an artist whose ability to write invigorating rock and perform it like no one else could not be outranked. *Purple Rain* became America's new Saturday night treat; in most places, you could see the movie several times for the same price as a one-time-only concert ticket. Many Prince fans went back to see the movie again and again, often emulating the Edwardian rock fashion that is Prince's trademark, bopping to the film's music, and reciting the dialogue with the fervor of acting students. Years from now, the movie will remain a cult favorite among rock music fans, not unlike the success of the '70's rock musical *The Rocky Horror Picture Show*.

An interesting fact has emerged as this story has been researched and written: no matter what people said or speculated about Prince, there still seems to be no shortage of respect and admiration for, devotion to, even outright idol worship of the man. There is, without a doubt, a special kind of reverence paid a person who says and does exactly what is on his mind.

Whether or not you can condone the methods he used to get what he wanted, no one can deny that Prince made it clear exactly *what* he wanted. He aimed his sights on being a superstar, and in the relatively short period of seven years, he became an international phenomenon. There is only one Prince. His vision, style and seemingly insatiable quest for the new has set bold standards in a world full of people afraid to march to their own beat.

It is just short of amazing to listen to the acts that Prince has influenced. There are many of them and all are proficient at re-creating Prince's sound—a synthesizer line here, a vocal pattern there. However, just when an imitator thinks they've discovered the secrets of the lyrics and music to songs like "Delirious" or "1999," Prince jumbles their senses with the artistry of "Automatic" or "When Doves Cry."

"'Purple Rain' is not the best thing Prince has got, not by a long shot," says Jesse Johnson. "He's got things recorded that are melodic; beautiful things he's done just sitting around.

I don't know if people are ready for that kind of stuff yet."

The crowd was more than ready for Prince that night after the premiere of *Purple Rain*. The Palace, a huge chic ballroom on Hollywood and Vine was packed to the walls with recognizable faces of movie stars and recording artists. It was obvious that some of these people had never even heard Prince's music before. "I thought the movie was all right, but I guess rock 'n' roll is just not my kind of music," actress Morgan Fairchild was overhead saying to a television reporter and crew.

Others were ecstatic. One tall, pretty blonde, who had had one drink too many, could not contain her excitement. "I think he is the greatest," she said to a girlfriend who seemed to be stargazing too heavily to even pay attention. "Don't you think he's sexy?" Her girlfriend didn't hear. The MTV camera scanned the party, in search of stars, and the cast of *Purple Rain* mingled with the crowd. Bob Cavallo and Joe Ruffalo worked the room of executives with their heads unusually high. Their peers there in the room would in several days read in the industry trades that *Purple Rain* had secured the management firm a movie production deal with Warner Bros. These were the same men who could not get arrested on a movie lot one year before. It *is* true that he who has the gold makes the rules. Cavallo, tuxedoed and gingerly sipping a cocktail, had something better than gold. He and his partners had *Prince*.

But where was Prince? This was his party, in his honor. The Prince of Hollywood was nowhere to be found. The strange and elusive Prince was again at work. In the room were some of the most powerful, beautiful and talented people in Los Angeles, but Prince didn't personally know *half* of them. If you're shy, you're shy—you don't suddenly snap out of it. Or perhaps Prince just wasn't impressed.

Instead, he asked to be ushered backstage, where he sat nervously, waiting to go on. It was supposed to be a secret, but after Sheila E. finished her set, Prince was going to perform three songs with The Revolution. Some secret. MTV had been talking about the party for days. Some fans had lined the front sidewalk of the Palace simply in hopes of *hearing* strains of something familiar to their ears.

Suddenly the curtain on the Palace stage began to rise, first bringing the loud chatter among this crowd to a muffled buzz, and then there was a roar. There he was, in all his rock 'n' roll majesty, all ruffled up and funky. Behind him, their images bleeding through the smoke, were members of The Revolution, instruments purring. The whole ensemble looked like a band of hip, renegade misfits. Prince took the microphone—didn't take it off its stand—just posed with it, moving his hip to the metronome groove of "17 Days."

Hollywood luminaries and waitresses alike were going crazy, and with good reason: this diminutive figure, too shy to face Christopher Reeve ten minutes before, was rocking the place off its foundation, incorporating vintage Jackie Wilson steps with hip juts and torrid pelvis action. When he sang "When Doves Cry"—the song everyone had been waiting for—Prince let loose a scream so piercing that it was clear that he could still feel the emotional effects of the haunting groove.

As mysteriously as it had begun, so had it ended, with Prince donating more excitement in a matter of minutes than anyone could imagine possible. They roared their approval, a pocket of patrons in one corner even attempted to get an encore.

But Prince wasn't even *there*. He stepped off the stage and into a limousine, and he was gone, his purple limousine cutting the brisk night air.

Discography

ALBUMS

For You, Warner Bros., BSK-3150. Released 4/7/78. This is Prince's very first album, the one his ex-manager Owen Husney fought so hard to have his artist produce. Certainly a more conventional production by comparison to his later work; even here one can detect an imaginative mind on the rise. Songs like "Soft and Wet" and "My Love Is Forever" are unbelievably Top-40ish ("Just as Long as We're Together" features a line, "I'll bring the music, you bring the wine"), but the sounds Prince gets on synthesizers and guitars suggested where he was going.

Prince, Warner Bros., BSK-3366. Released 10/19/79. Technically this album stood head and shoulders over his debut, and musically Prince had begun melding those lyrical chords with incredible grooves. One of them, the mighty "Sexy Dancer," is the essence of what Prince is all about today: erotic lyrics over a relentless rhythm track that features a tasty acoustic piano solo. It is interesting to note that in the artist's first two albums, it is difficult to recognize that Prince, at heart, is a guitar player first and a keyboardist second; these productions are dominated by various synthesizers.

Dirty Mind, Warner Bros., BSK 3478. Released 10/15/80. What could have been a commercial tragedy turned out to be an artistic landmark. Aside from *1999* and *Purple Rain*, *Dirty Mind* is probably the most important work in the musician's career, considering the fact that here, Prince takes freedom of speech to the extreme. During the title track, Prince proclaims, "I have a dirty mind," before easing into the subject of incest during the frenzied "Sister," dancing his way through the funky "Head," but finding a pocket during the stride of "Partyup." By now, Prince was certainly on his way.

Controversy, Warner Bros., BSK 3601. Released 10/14/81. Having gotten away with the provocative *Dirty Mind*, Prince continues his groove-and-shock tactic during this LP. Here, Prince introduced monologue to his tracks, dealing not so much with blatant sexual themes as national burdens (gun control during "Annie Christian"; nuclear war during "Ronnie, Talk to Russia"). Important tracks: the driving vamp of "Let's Work" (for real frenzy, try the 12-inch version), the rebellion of "Sexuality" and of course, the title track, which really spurred controversy with Prince's narration of The Lord's Prayer.

1999, Warner Bros., 1-23720. Released 10/27/82. The album every recording artist prays for in his career. *Purple Rain* is Prince's greatest success to date, but *1999* is what got him there (for Michael Jackson, it was the brilliant *Off the Wall*), and despite *Rain*'s commercial and artistic glory, it is *1999* that is the essential Prince. It is almost a crime that Prince included so many great tracks on this two-record set, things like the quirky "Automatic," "Little Red Corvette," the modern rockabilly of "Delirious" and the psychotic dance anthem "D.M.S.R. (Dance Music Sex Romance)." "All the Critics Love U in New York," Prince coos. A bold statement perhaps, but after hearing the torch ballad "International Lover" and the punchy "Lady Cab Driver," most of them agreed.

Purple Rain, Warner Bros., 1-25110. Released 6/25/84. Prince's crowning success and the soundtrack from the movie of the same name. The great thing about the record is each track holds up on its own. Absent is any "atmosphere" music that producers always deem worthy of soundtrack LPs. The production's first single, "When Doves Cry," knocked our socks off with its blunt, unconventional style. There's not even a bass line here—just a synthesizer, drum machine, some penetrating guitar, and at the center of it all, Prince's intense, emotional lead vocal. An even bigger success as a single was the accessible, straight-ahead rock 'n' roll of "Let's Go Crazy," a track whose energy is rivaled only by the joyous gospel of "Baby, I'm a Star." Collectively not as powerful an album as *1999*, but even when Prince goes Madison Avenue, he's miles ahead of the rest.

IMPORTANT SINGLES

Essential to the Prince collection are songs released as B sides of singles, in either 7- or 12-inch format, that didn't appear on Prince albums. B sides are listed first.

"How Come U Don't Call Me Anymore," "1999," Warner Bros., 7-29896B, released 9/22/82.

"Horny Toad," '"Delirious," Warner Bros., 7-29503, released 8/23/83.

"Irresistible Bitch," "Let's Pretend We're Married," Warner Bros., 7-29548, released 11/23/83.

"17 Days (The rain will come down, then U will have 2 choose. If U believe, look 2 the dawn and U shall never lose)," "When Doves Cry," Warner Bros., 7-29286, released 5/16/84.

"Erotic City," "Let's Go Crazy," Warner Bros., 7-29216, released 7/18/84.

IMPORTANT TRACKS FROM PRINCE PRODUCTIONS

"Cool," "Get It Up," '"The Stick" from *The Time*, Warner Bros., released 4/81.

"The Walk," "Wild and Loose," '"777-9311," and "Gigolos Get Lonely, Too," from *What Time Is It*, The Time, released 8/82.

"Jungle Love" and "The Bird," from *Ice Cream Castles*, The Time, Warner Bros., released 7/84.

"Nasty Girl," "Drive Me Wild," and "If a Girl Answers (Don't Hang Up)" from *Vanity 6*, Warner Bros., released 8/82.